Time of the Vulture

How to Survive the Crisis and Prosper in the Process

By Darryl Robert Schoon

"The air's going bad."

"What do you mean, the air's going bad?"

"The sky's not blue. It's dirty and turning brown and there's more."

"There's more?"

"The water's not too good either and something's wrong with the weather."

"The air's bad, the water's not good either, and something's wrong with the weather. Next, you're going to say something's wrong with our money."

"Well, now that you've brought it up…"

When stocks lose their value

That's a terrible thing

When homes lose their value

That's a terrible thing

But when money loses its value

That's the most terrible thing of all

TABLE OF CONTENTS

PREFACE

Introduction

SECTION I

Time of the Vulture, the story of the hare, the tortoise, the ostrich and the vulture; Real estate and global financial markets; Understanding complex markets; Threat of rising interest rates

The world that once was is no longer; History of the US dollar; What happened to America's gold; President Eisenhower warns America; Eisenhower's warning ignored

Sand dollars and the approach of the vulture; US refuses to back US dollars; US, OPEC, and the dollar as a world reserve currency; End of the dollar era; Vulnerability of the dollar

Foreign exchange markets and value of money; Speculators and US dollar; Instability and profits: betting on money

Betting on the US dollar; Bond trader Bill Gross; similarities between GM and the US; When reserve currencies are in trouble; Asian assets, Asian currencies

Alan Greenspan; Greenspan's warning; Greenspan's warning overridden; Consequences of overriding Greenspan's warning; Green-spin

SECTION II

SECTION III

SECTION V

SECTION VI

SECTION VIII

ADDENDA LIST

<u>CARTOONS</u>

PREFACE TO 2012 EDITION

In April 2006, fellow Positive Deviant Network member John Botti (former global head of Credit Lyonnais Credit Management, a multi-billion dollar proprietary hedge fund) and I discussed our concerns about the future of the US economy.

For years, I had harbored deep misgivings about the US economy and John's concerns caused me to collect my thoughts on the subject. It is now eleven months later and my paper on the impending financial crisis—*How to Survive the Crisis and Prosper in the Process*—is complete.

It is my hope it will help members of the Positive Deviant Network and others to understand what is now about to happen. The US and global economy are on very thin ice and it is best you know this and understand why it is so. If you do, you may be able to protect yourself and your loved ones from the economic devastation that is about to occur.

It is my deepest wish that you will be able to do so.

Take care and good luck.

Darryl Robert Schoon
Member, The Positive Deviant Network
February 2007

2012 Update

In 2006, I wrote *The Time of the Vulture: How To Survive the Crisis and Prosper in the Process* and in March 2007 I submitted it to a private network of 'out-of-the-box thinkers' called the Positive Deviant Network.

Soon after, the crisis I predicted began to happen; and, now, in 2012 the crisis has entered a far more dangerous stage. Despite historic levels of central bank intervention and trillions of dollars of money borrowed and spent, the economic collapse has resumed and is gathering speed.

When I wrote my book in 2006/2007, it was not known then whether the Fed would keep interest rates high or would lower them. Either way, the consequences would be significant as interest rates are the key to liquidity in credit-based economies; and are the primary tool in maintaining the critical balance between credit and debt necessary in capitalist economies.

By cutting interest rates in 2008, the Fed hoped cheap credit would revive the damaged global economy and overcome the momentum of increasing levels of defaulting debt then underway. It didn't.

While low central bank interest rates and unprecedented levels of government money did prevent an immediate economic collapse; that respite has come at the cost of even greater financial damage in the future.

Today, a deflationary collapse is gathering momentum. The ability to pay down existing debt is diminishing as the levels of debt grow ever larger; and the added trillions of debt borrowed and spent in the attempt to contain the debt crisis has added even more debt to the debts that cannot even now be repaid.

The 1930s now loom ever larger in the suppressed fears of central bankers. Their belief they had the tools and understanding to prevent another Great Depression has been shaken. Despite everything they have done since 2008, they have been unable to revive the US and global economy.

The unprecedented liquidity and money creation used to slow the collapse is now circulating in the global economy. This massive liquidity will eventually cause widespread currency debasement, inflation and possible hyperinflation.

When I started writing *The Time of the Vulture* the price of gold was $600. Since then, the price of gold has tripled and will go even higher as more paper money is printed in capitalism's death spiral. Invented in China 1,000 years ago, paper money caused the collapse of four dynasties in five hundred years. Today, more governments will fall.

Since 2007, much of what I predicted has happened and, yet, the crisis is not yet over. The events I foresaw then are still in motion today, albeit 5 years closer to their inevitable and cataclysmic resolution.

What follows is an analysis of economic conditions prior to the economic collapse in 2008. This edition, the 3rd edition of Time of the Vulture, 2012, contains updates where needed. In Addendum VI, *It Will Get Better; But, First, It's Going To Get Worse*, I will discuss what this crisis is all about. It's not just about money.

Preface

SECTION I

TIME OF THE VULTURE

Topic 1

In times of expansion, it is to the hare the prizes go. Quick, risk taking, and bold, his qualities are exactly suited to the times. In periods of contraction, the tortoise is favored. Slow and conservative, quick only to retract his vulnerable head and neck, his is the wisest bet when the slow and sure is preferable to the quick and easy.

Every so often, however, there comes a time when neither the hare nor the tortoise is the victor. This is when both the bear and the bull have been vanquished, when the pastures upon which the bull once grazed are long gone and the bear's lair itself lies buried deep beneath the rubble of economic collapse.

This is the time of the vulture, for the vulture feeds neither upon the pastures of the bull nor the stored up wealth of the bear. The vulture feeds instead upon the blind ignorance and denial of the ostrich. The time of the vulture is at hand.

The Time of the Vulture is not just a story. It is a story whose time has come. And if you understand why the story is true, you will be able to protect yourself and profit in the chaotic days ahead. If you do not, you will play the ostrich in a story that will soon affect us all, rich and poor, bull and bear, ostrich and vulture alike.

When investing, people do not choose to be bulls or bears. Being risk taking or risk adverse is often due to personality. But people do choose to be ostriches, especially in times of change. This is because denial of change—the refuge of the ostrich—gives all of us a sense of security. Though the security is as false as the comfort it offers, unfortunately many, if not most of us, will choose to be ostriches in the days ahead.

5

WHO WILL BE THE OSTRICHES?

- Those who resist change, insisting that what was true yesterday will be true tomorrow.

- Those who do not understand that we are in the midst of the mother of all paradigm shifts, a shift so fundamental the world of tomorrow will bear little resemblance to the world of today.

- Those who have been so financially successful in the current paradigm, they will not realize the world has changed until too late.

The line separating investment and speculation, which is never bright and clear, becomes blurred still further when most market participants have recently enjoyed triumphs. Nothing sedates rationality like large doses of effortless money. After a heady experience of that kind, normally sensible people drift into behavior akin to that of Cinderella at the ball. They know that overstaying the festivities - that is, continuing to speculate in companies that have gigantic valuations relative to the cash they are likely to generate in the future - will eventually bring on pumpkins and mice. But they nevertheless hate to miss a single minute of what is one helluva party. Therefore, the giddy participants all plan to leave just seconds before midnight. There's a problem, though: They are dancing in a room in which the clocks have no hands.
- Warren Buffet, Berkshire Hathaway 2000 Annual Report

UNDERSTANDING TODAY'S COMPLEX FINANCIAL MARKETS

If you can understand your local real estate market you can understand what is happening to global financial markets. Although mortgages and multiple listings have little in common with derivative swaps and tranches, what collapsed US real estate markets also collapsed global financial markets. Prices of both local real estate and global financial markets collapsed because of rising interest rates.

FALLING AND RISING INTEREST RATES AND GLOBAL BUBBLES

The US housing boom (2002-2005) was created by low interest rates. The reasons for the low interest rates are as misunderstood as are the reasons for our current crisis.

The Lord giveth and the Lord taketh away. Well, regarding home purchases from 2002-2005, the Lord did give, in the form of low interest rates; however, from 2005-2007, the Lord then took back the low interest rates.

This is why interest rates were lowered in 2002-2005:

After the collapse of the dot.com bubble in 2000, a policy of easy credit was instituted by the US Federal Reserve to keep the US from slipping into a deflationary (low demand) cycle as happened after the 1929 stock market crash. That deflationary cycle became known as the Great Depression.

The Fed was also aware that the more recent 1989 crash of the Japanese stock market had plunged Japan into its own deflationary cycle. When the dot.com stock bubble burst in March of 2000, deflation in the US (the world's largest economy), in addition to a still continuing deflation in Japan (the world's 2nd largest economy), was far too dangerous to allow.

A simultaneous deflation in both the US and Japan would inevitably spread to the rest of the world and cause another depression. The solution chosen by the US and the Japanese Central Banks was to flood their economies with easy credit. Central Bank interest rates in the US were cut to 1 % and Japanese rates were already slashed at 0 % -- in reality a negative interest rate because of constant inflationary monetary growth.

This flood of easy credit temporarily had the desired effect; and the US, reinvigorated by this flood of cheap credit, managed to stay afloat thanks to a housing boom and a new bubble set in motion by the low 1 % interest rates.

Japan's descent into its 15-year deflationary cycle was also slowed. There, the flood of Japanese yen reinvigorated not only its moribund banking system, but, more importantly, inadvertently fueled a worldwide boom in financial markets.

With 0 % interest rates in Japan, it was believed only a fool could not make money investing at that rate (and no investment banker has ever believed him/herself to be a fool). From these 0 % interest rates a heretofore unknown monetary phenomenon known as the Japanese yen carry-trade became the primary engine of worldwide financial speculation.

Borrowing Japanese yen cheap and investing in anything that promised higher returns became the game of choice for the world financial community, producing hundreds of billions of dollars in profits for investment banks and speculators from 2002-2007.

By April 2006, the flood of easy credit had driven prices in all markets (housing, stocks, bonds, commodities, derivatives, etc.) to multi-year highs. But in 2005, central banks began raising interest rates to contain inflationary pressures set in motion by their previously low rates.

With interest rates rising, in May 2006 the US stock market began to falter with the Dow suffering multi-100 plus losses and emerging markets took the biggest hit of all, losing an estimated $5 billion of value in a week.

From mid-May to mid-June '06, the total loss for world stock markets was $2 trillion. The financial bubble created by low interest rates had peaked. The central bank policy of easy credit ended in 2005 and the higher interest rates began to deflate the bubbles that low interest rates had created.

Easy credit not only led to higher asset prices but also to higher prices in general, i.e. inflation; and to combat inflation, the only weapon of Central Banks is to raise interest rates. This is where local real estate markets and global financial markets had the same problem.

Because their purchases and profits were both based on the availability of low interest loans, home buyers and investment bankers were equally vulnerable to the rise of interest rates in 2005. Prices always depend on buyers and when buyers depend on credit and credit becomes dear, prices collapse.

When I first wrote my analysis of the US and global economy in 2006/2007, it was not known what central bankers would then do to combat rising prices. The central banks knew their low interest rates had ignited inflationary pressures and the usual response would be to raise rates. But they also knew that the economies could collapse if interest rates were raised too far too fast.

Twenty-five years ago, in a like time of economic insecurity, the US Central Bank had raised interest rates from 8 % to 21.5 % to bring inflation under control. At the time, I had a $400,000 bank line of credit and dealt in a luxury item, fine hand-knotted Chinese carpets.

When interest rates skyrocketed, suddenly wall to wall carpeting and linoleum flooring didn't look so bad. I and many others went out of business and inflation was brought under control. Today, the environment is very different.

Now, public, private, and business indebtedness is at an all-time high. The Reagan years ushered in a mentality of borrow now, make payments forever, and never pay anything off. The prevailing mantra has become refinance, refinance, refinance. This became true for governments, families, and businesses.

If interest rates were raised as they were in the past, the economic carnage would now be far greater. And if interest rates were not raised, inflation could turn virulent and the flow of foreign moneys upon which the US depends could abruptly halt.

We now know in 2012 what was not known in 2007, whether central banks would raise interest rates to combat inflation or would lower rates to keep the global economy afloat. The subsequent credit contraction and collapse of investment banks in 2007/2008 intervened to force central banks to again lower interest rates, hoping to prevent a deflationary collapse that could usher in another Great

Depression.

Now in 2012, the collapse of real estate, stocks and commodities has wiped out trillions of dollars of wealth and it is deflationary, not inflationary, pressures that threaten central bankers. A deflationary collapse today, however, will be more painful than even the Great Depression because today debt levels are far higher than in the 1930s.

This deflationary collapse will not be another cyclical correction. This deflationary collapse will be an omega event, a one-time event of unprecedented proportions that will alter the global economic, political, and social landscape—and, to understand why this will be, you must first understand what happened to the US dollar after 1950.

> **2012 UPDATE:** Today's excessive money printing combined with historically low interest rates will eventually debase all currencies. Central bankers are hoping before this happens, economies will recover. They won't.

THE WORLD THAT ONCE WAS IS NO LONGER

Topic 2

History is the story of change. We have all changed. We are not what we once were though part of us still believes we are. So it is with the US and US dollar. It too is not what it once was, though many of us still believe it is. For years, the US was the wealthiest nation in the world and the US dollar was the symbol of financial stability and security. And so it was.

In 1950 the US was the world's only creditor nation; it was the world's bank and the US dollar was the world's reserve currency. Fifty-six years later, a sea change in the fortunes of the US and the US dollar has occurred. But most Americans do not understand the magnitude and significance of this change. Soon, they will.

To understand what has happened, you will first need a short history lesson. Understanding what happened to the US dollar is no more complicated than understanding interest rates. The lesson as to what happened to the US dollar, however, is much more consequential.

History can be boring when it's not relevant. However, this time it's different. Whether you know it or not, the history of the US dollar is very relevant; for what has happened to the US dollar will soon impact you in same way Hurricane Katrina impacted the residents of New Orleans.

THE RECENT HISTORY OF THE US DOLLAR

In 1949, the US dollar was the strongest currency in the world. Fully backed by gold and convertible at $35 per ounce, the US dollar functioned as the world's reserve currency. At the time, the US owned 21,775 metric tons of gold, 75 % of the world's monetary gold, the largest tonnage and largest percentage ever held by any one nation in history.

That was when every American school child knew about Fort Knox and the gold that was stored there. But today's school children aren't told about Fort Knox. This is not because America's teachers are failing to teach school children about America's wealth. It's because the vast majority of that gold is gone, sold to pay down America's debts; and, the gold that remains is there only because in 1971 the US refused to pay the rest of the gold it owed.

HISTORY IS NOT JUST WHAT YOU KNOW
HISTORY ALSO INCLUDES WHAT YOU DON'T KNOW

Although the US owned 21,775 metric tons of gold in 1949, by 1970, the US had only 7,200 tons left [estimated as no actual figures available]. And with only 7,200 tons, the US still owed 38,879 tons, a negative net 31,679 tons.

In only 21 years, the US went from owning 21,775 tons of gold to owing 31,679 tons, an outflow of 53,454 metric tons of the most precious metal on earth. How much gold does the US now actually have? No one knows because since 1954 the US has refused to allow a public physical audit of its gold.

Fort Knox

I know your next question:

WHERE DID ALL THE GOLD GO?

The answer:

AMERICA'S GOLD PAID FOR TWENTY-ONE YEARS OF U.S. OVERSEAS MILITARY EXPENDITURES, TWO U.S. OVERSEAS WARS, AND TO FUND TWENTY ONE YEARS OF U.S. OVERSEAS CORPORATE EXPANSION.

> *The decline of great powers is caused by simple economic over extension.*
> - Paul Kennedy The Rise and Fall of the Great Powers

It should be noted that prior to the US reneging on its international monetary obligations in 1971, gold transfers between nations were determined solely by international currency flows. Prior to 1971, if a country bought more goods than it sold, it would transfer gold bullion or the equivalent in US dollars ($35 per ounce of gold) to other countries. If a country exported more than it imported, it would instead receive gold or its equivalent in US dollars.

Because the US, then the most advanced industrial power in the world, had a positive trade balance between 1949 and 1970, US gold supplies should have increased. The fact that US gold reserves instead disappeared is evidence of the vast amounts of money the US military and US corporations spent abroad during that time.

From 1949 to 1970, maintaining a worldwide military presence, fighting wars in Korea and Vietnam, and underwriting US corporate overseas expansion completely drained the US Treasury of its gold. During this period, the US spent more than twice the amount of gold it actually possessed.

A ROAD NOT TAKEN

This disappearance of America's gold went unnoticed by Americans. This fact points out a deeply denied truth about our nation—that our collective awareness is not as free as we wish to believe.

Our collective awareness, in fact, is managed by those in government who wish us to see what they would have us see and to believe what they would have us believe. Crowd control, not the dissemination of much needed truths to a democratic electorate, is the policy of the US government.

Something as important as the disappearance of America's patrimony, its wealth, its collective storehouse of value, its gold, should have been noticed. If a large bank heist occurs, this makes the news. When the stock market falls, it makes the news. But when America's wealth, its gold, is gone and spent, there's nothing about in the news.

AMERICA DIDN'T NOTICE BECAUSE AMERICANS WEREN'T TOLD

Well, that's not quite true. Americans were warned and by someone quite important. Though Americans weren't warned specifically about the gold, Americans were warned about the powerful interests sending US dollars abroad at such a rate that America's gold would soon disappear.

As an indication of how powerful these interests are, the man who warned America, Dwight D. Eisenhower, was the President of the United States and informed the nation of what was occurring only as he was about to leave office because of the dangers of so doing.

> *The real rulers in Washington are invisible, and exercise power from behind the scenes.*
> - Felix Frankfurter, US Supreme Court Justice

President Eisenhower warned America three days before his term ended; and, it was then he felt safe enough to name those responsible. He called them ***"the military-industrial complex"***, a collusion of military and business interests so powerful that unless opposed, Eisenhower believed they posed a threat not only to America's wealth but also to its freedoms. In his farewell speech to the nation in 1961, the highly decorated and retired General warned:

> *This conjunction of an immense military establishment and a large arms industry is new in the American experience. The total influence -- economic, political, even spiritual -- is felt in every city, every State house, every office of the Federal government. We recognize the imperative need for this development. Yet we must not fail to comprehend its grave implications. Our toil, resources and livelihood are all involved; so is the very structure of our society.*

> *In the councils of government, we must guard against the acquisition of unwarranted influence, whether sought or unsought, by the military-industrial complex. The potential for the disastrous rise of misplaced power exists and will persist.*

> *...We cannot mortgage the material assets of our grandchildren without risking the loss also of their political and spiritual heritage. We want democracy to survive for all generations to come, not to become the insolvent phantom of tomorrow.*

Eisenhower's warnings went unheeded. And just as he predicted, the US is now insolvent and the material assets of our grandchildren have been mortgaged beyond their ability and even their grandchildren's ability to repay. The national debt of the US stands now at $10.9 trillion and is growing at a rate of almost $100 million each hour.

> *No generation has a right to contract debts greater than can be paid off during the course of its own existence.*
>
> - George Washington 1789

It is not our purpose here to otherwise detail what occurred as a result of Eisenhower's unheeded warning, other than the loss of America's gold. For those interested, the works of the late Professor Seymour Melman of Columbia University will be more than enough to satisfy your interest regarding the effect of the US military-industrial complex on America. It is our purpose here only to increase your understanding of the grave danger you are now facing as a result of what has already occurred.

> **2012 UPDATE:** In 2007, US debt was $10.9 trillion and growing slightly less than $100 million per hour. Today, July 2012, US debt is $15.88 trillion (45% higher than in 2007) and is increasing at the rate of $162 million every hour.

A HOUSE BUILT ON SAND
SAND DOLLARS AND THE APPROACH
OF THE VULTURE

Topic 3

It was as if someone removed a pin from the axle of international commerce when the US dollar was no longer convertible to gold. Previously, the US dollar was linked to gold, and other currencies were linked to the dollar. Everything was stable. It is no longer so. Once the pin connecting gold and paper money was removed, everything changed. The axle of international commerce began to vibrate and lately it's been getting much worse. The fear is that the wheels are now about to come off.

Under the terms of the Bretton-Woods agreement in 1944, the US agreed to anchor the world currency system with the US dollar, a responsibility that also came with many privileges. Under that agreement, the US would link the dollar to gold and all other nations would link their currencies to the US dollar.

The amount of US dollars in circulation would be tied to the amount of gold the US owned, set at a ratio of 35 US dollars per ounce of gold possessed. The linking of the US dollar to gold and linking the dollar to other currencies gave a much needed stability to international trade and commerce.

When the US began sending its gold overseas to pay for the costs of its military and corporate overseas expansion and wars, the erosion of the US dollar began in earnest. By 1970, US gold holdings were actually negative—the US owed 38,879 tons of gold.

At that time, based on the negative US gold holdings, theoretically, all US dollars should have been recalled from circulation—and should have been long before then under the terms of Bretton-Woods.

Of course, this was not going to happen. As the world's largest economy and militarily the most powerful nation on earth, the US instead refused to exchange gold for its dollars and in 1973 officially and unilaterally announced that the US dollar was no longer convertible. US Treasury Secretary John Connolly stated, "The US dollar may be our currency but it's your problem."

WHEN A POOR MAN DEFAULTS HE LOSES EVERYTHING WHEN A RICH MAN DEFAULTS EVERYONE ELSE LOSES SOMETHING

It is important to know that when the US refused in 1971 to convert US dollars to gold, it was the first time in history a world reserve currency was not backed by either gold or silver. (A reserve currency is the predominant currency in which world trade is conducted).

A reserve currency convertible to gold or silver gives buyers and sellers the needed confidence that they are trading their goods for more than paper money. In 1971, when the US first refused to convert dollars to gold, the confidence offered by a convertible reserve currency was no more. This uncertainty, this lack of confidence in paper money, is now the single greatest threat to the stability of the world financial system.

The decision to de-link the US dollar from gold was not made by a panel of expert economists who, after much debate, concluded gold no longer had a place in modern finance. The decision to de-link the US dollar from gold was made only because the US no longer had gold to back the dollar.

With the dollar no longer convertible to gold, the US had to find other reasons for countries to continue using the US dollar as a reserve currency. The reserve currency status of US dollar gives the US an extraordinary advantage over others. It could issue debt in US dollars that others must repay only with dollars and in regards to its own expenses, it need merely print more dollars and refinance. No other country could do the same on such a scale.

The question became: how was the US dollar going to continue as the world's reserve currency when it was no longer convertible to gold? Where was the incentive to hold the US paper-dollar going to come from? The answer was to be found in the Middle East.

OPEC is a cartel, a monopoly that sets its prices not on market conditions but by what is commonly called "price-fixing". This serves the purposes of the US because OPEC has required payment for oil in US dollars. This requirement forced all countries to keep significant reserves of US dollars in order to pay for oil. However as compelling a reason as this is, it was to be only temporary.

In 1999, Europe issued its new currency, the euro, and in 2000, President Saddam Hussein announced Iraq would accept only euros, not US dollars for its oil and Venezuela is considering doing the same. However, in 2003, the US invaded Iraq, and one of the first things it did was to switch payment for Iraqi oil back to dollars.

Additionally, Iran has announced that it will create an oil exchange in which its oil will be offered only in euros, not dollars. And in June 2006, Russia's stock exchange began trading oil, oil products, and gold not in dollars or euros, but in rubles.

You may be asking:

WHAT DOES THIS MEAN?

You should be asking:

WHAT DOES THIS MEAN TO YOU?

But you should really be asking:

WHAT DOES THIS MEAN TO OTHERS?

Why?

BECAUSE IT IS OTHERS WHO WILL DECIDE
WHAT YOUR DOLLARS WILL SOON BE WORTH

2012 UPDATE: In 2012, the European debt crisis has exerted downward pressure on the euro causing the US dollar to temporarily appear to be a 'safe-haven'. While in the past, it was true, it is no longer. The reflexive rush to the US dollar will someday prove fatal. No paper currency including the US dollar will survive this economic cycle, at least in their present form.

THE TIME OF THE VULTURE DRAWS NEAR

Topic 4

When the value of money
Is determined by gamblers
Intent on short term gain
The end is not too far away

Prior to the US de-linking the dollar from gold, foreign exchange markets existed solely to facilitate international commerce. If, for example, a merchant wanted to buy Russian grain and its price was set in rubles, the merchant would purchase rubles on the foreign exchange market and exchange those rubles for the grain. However, after 1973, when the US officially ended the convertibility of the US dollar to gold, the foreign exchange markets were never to be the same.

In 1974, the foreign exchange markets took on a completely new role. With the US dollar no longer backed by gold and with all currencies previously linked to the dollar, what were currencies now worth? What was the US dollar worth? And, what was the relative value between currencies? Between the US dollar and the British pound? Between the Russian ruble and the Japanese yen? Between the US dollar and the Italian lira, the French franc, the Spanish peseta and the Chinese yuan?

In the absence of any real value, it was now left to speculators in the foreign exchange markets to fill the breach, to determine the actual and relative value of currencies upon which world trade depended. And, whereas producers, manufacturers, and farmers along with those who purchase and sell those products desire stable currencies in order to maintain orderly markets, speculators desire the very opposite. For it is in the swings between high and low the speculator takes his greatest profits; the greater the swings the greater the profits, the lower the swings the lower the profits.

The de-linking of the US dollar from gold had inadvertently opened the doors of world commerce to a completely new guest, gamblers and speculators in the form of investment bankers who much prefer to call themselves financial services providers in polite company.

There are those who say that speculators have always played a key role in the markets, performing a needed function in smoothing out the inevitable wrinkles between highs and lows. And, to a degree, there is truth in this. Both producers and buyers would use the forward markets to hedge their bets as to next year's prices—prices affected by uncertainties such as weather, war, or the various other sundries that affect human endeavor.

But today's investment bankers do not have the same vested interest in the markets that producers and buyers have. Today's investment bankers have only one interest—not to protect the continuing ability to profitably produce and distribute, but only to maximize short term profit and gain. Instability, not stability, is the desired playground of the new guest.

After 1974, the nature of foreign exchange markets changed dramatically. Foreign exchange markets, now commonly known as FX or forex markets, are today primarily speculative in nature with speculation accounting for over 98 % of total volume.

From insignificant numbers in 1974 and now $3 to $4 trillion per day, the volume of bets wagered on the relative value of tomorrow's money has grown exponentially. As it has grown, so, too, has the danger to the US paper dollar.

THE US DOLLAR
AN AGING HORSE IN DECLINING
HEALTH HOPING AGAINST HOPE
TO DEFY THE ODDS
THE SPECULATORS ARE PLACING THEIR
BETS NOW

Topic 5

Bond traders are by nature a conservative lot. Buying debt instead of equity they look more closely at a customer's ability to repay than his ability to expand. If otherwise, they would find themselves on the equity side of the equation where bets are placed on promise and hope, not on character and collateral.

Bill Gross is not a widely known public figure. In some circles, however, his name is as well known as it is respected. There, Bill Gross is known for his role as Managing Director of the PIMCO bond fund, the largest bond fund in the US. Managing over $680 billion dollars in assets, Bill Gross is considered by many to be the most influential bond trader in the world.

In his May 2006 PIMCO Investment Outlook, Bill Gross drew the comparison between the US and General Motors. That comparison could just as well have been done fifty years ago with very different results. In the 1950s, the US and General Motors were at the top of their respective categories. The US was the wealthiest, most powerful nation in the world; GM the world's largest manufacturer, a profitable expanding enterprise with the world's largest market share for automobiles.

Today, similarities between the two remain but for very different reasons. Both are now heavily indebted with high fixed costs and long term obligations, obligations that will be difficult to repay, especially in the face of a declining market share for GM and for the US, a ballooning negative trade balance, the loss of its manufacturing base, and the largest debt of any nation in history. Today, a troubled future faces both.

Of the current similarities between the US and GM, Gross noted:

> *I think it is important to recognize that General Motors is a canary in this country's economic coal mine; a forerunner for what's to come for the broader economy. Their mistakes have resembled this nation's mistakes; their problems will be our future problems.*

He then enumerated three problem areas now shared by the US and GM:

(1) Declining global competitiveness
(2) Uncompetitive labor costs compared to global competition
(3) Burdensome future liabilities—pensions and healthcare

Of particular interest is what Bill Gross predicted the US might do regarding its "burdensome future liabilities", which include an $8.37 trillion ever-growing mountain of government debt.

> *How are we to pay for this future burden of healthcare and social security expenses? Aside from contractual legislative changes to both areas (which are surely just around the corner), the way a reserve currency nation gets out from under the burden of excessive liabilities is to inflate, devalue, and tax.*

Mr. Gross's last phrase bears repeating:

> <u>*the way a reserve currency nation gets out from*</u>
> <u>*under the burden of excessive liabilities is to*</u>
> <u>*inflate, devalue, and tax.*</u>

Got that? Good.

INFLATE, DEVALUE, AND TAX

Just wanted to make sure. Gross then went on to conclude:

> *Higher inflation, higher personal and corporate taxes, and a lower dollar point U.S. and global investors away from U.S. assets and toward more competitive economies less burdened by health and pension liabilities – those personified by higher savings rates and investment as a percentage of GDP.* **Need I say more than to sell U.S. assets and buy Asian ones denominated in their local currencies; or if necessary to hire a global asset manager with sufficient flexibility and proper foresight to thrive in an increasingly difficult investment environment?**

SELL US ASSETS
BUY ASIAN ASSETS IN ASIAN CURRENCIES

Bill Gross spoke what is now on the mind of money managers across the globe. Money managers do not earn their multi-million dollar salaries by staying in markets too long or for the wrong reasons. Yesterday's yield determines today's paycheck and tomorrow's job.

If you are to survive in what even Bill Gross calls "an increasingly difficult investment environment", if you are to prosper, it is absolutely necessary you understand who is in the game, what they are going to do (or might do) and what exactly your options are.

You are not as powerful as the government. You are not as rich and as quick as those who control billions in their search for return. You are, however, going to need every resource you can gather about you as we approach what I call "the rupture".

Prayer, by the way, is not a bad place to start. Faith will be hard to come by in the days ahead and will be more valuable than gold—and gold is going to be very, very, very valuable.

ALAN GREENSPAN KBE

Topic 6

One of the saddest lessons of history is this: If we've been bamboozled long enough, we tend to reject any evidence of the bamboozle. The bamboozle has captured us. Once you give a charlatan power over you, you almost never get it back.

- Carl Sagan

In the parsing of a man, or in fact, of anything, the human mind attempts to draw a conclusion. Not always easy and not always appropriate, a man's life and actions are oftentimes no more compatible to judgment than anything else in God's creation. In this, Alan Greenspan is no exception.

Called "the maestro" by admirers for his apparent ability to orchestrate today's complex markets, Alan Greenspan occupies a special niche in the history of modern finance. In 2002, Greenspan was made an honorary knight by England's Queen Elizabeth, who awarded him a medal making Greenspan a Knight of the British Empire.

Although not able to refer to himself as "Sir Alan", the letters KBE can nonetheless be appended to his name; a significant award at the very least. For the good doctor Greenspan did indeed give valued service to those he served, though it was not you or I or the American people whose interests "the maestro" ultimately served; it was those closest to the spigot, the spigot of credit that first fills the troughs of those closest to it.

One decade ago, in 1996, as Chairman of the US Federal Reserve Bank, Greenspan was well aware of the figures then coming across his desk and those of his fellow Fed Governors. The figures were disturbing, raising alarm bells especially in the minds of those trained to understand their significance.

In the fall of 1996, the US stock markets were in danger of overheating. The Dow had risen 80 % in 26 months. Flows of US dollars were returning to the US to be invested in the New York Stock Exchange and NASDAQ in ever greater numbers, driving share prices ever higher and, as they rose, attracting more and more dollars which in turn again drove prices higher than before—a merry-go-round as it were, a merry-go-round of potential disaster upon which all of us, investors, observers, and bystanders alike were riding.

To those who studied and understood what the numbers meant, the figures pointed to the formation of a speculative bubble, a bubble that if allowed to grow, could endanger the world economy and the well-being of all. It was also a speculative bubble that Greenspan thought they had pricked two years earlier, in 1994.

> *I think we partially broke the back of an emerging speculation in equities... We pricked this bubble as well, I think.*
> - Alan Greenspan, February 1994

But the bubble was stronger than they had believed. So two years later, in October 1996, Greenspan did what he had to do; he warned Congress a bubble was in the making:

> *...how do we know when irrational exuberance has unduly escalated asset values, which then become subject to unexpected and prolonged contractions as they have in Japan over the past decade?*

For those who read the text of Greenspan's 1996 speech in its entirety, one can easily see Greenspan's careful attempts to lay the groundwork for an extraordinarily important and well-crafted argument; his warning that if present economic conditions were allowed to continue, a stock market bubble and collapse could occur in the US as it recently had in Japan, now in a deflationary cycle. The collapse of another large speculative bubble could lead to a deflationary depression and Greenspan knew it.

Four months later with irrational exuberance still driving stock prices higher, in February 1997 Greenspan repeated his warning, threatening this time to raise interest rates if the markets did not respond:

Given the lags with which monetary policy affects the economy, we cannot rule out a situation in which a preemptive policy tightening may become appropriate before any sign of actual higher inflation becomes evident.

This time, with Greenspan's threat to raise interest rates, the markets responded, as the International Herald Tribune on February 27, 1997, reported:

In Blunt Testimony, Greenspan Talks of Inflation Concerns: Fed Message On Rates Sends Stocks Tumbling

The Dow Jones dropped more than 115 points after Greenspan's testimony. The next day the Dow dropped another 55 and bond prices suffered even more. Greenspan's warning was definitely heard by Wall Street, the good doctor's medicine was working, irrational exuberance was on the retreat.

But the investment community was not to be denied. The 80 % run-up in two years had whetted their appetites. The Dow had risen steadily for a decade and was now picking up momentum. There was blood in the water, they knew it and they wanted more. A phone call was made from Wall Street to Greenspan's masters or perhaps a personal visit took place. Whatever action occurred, it was effective.

The next month, March 1997, Alan Greenspan made his capitulation speech to Wall Street, stating clearly for all to hear and confirming for once and for all that Alan Greenspan, Chairman of the US Federal Reserve, was but a prestigious paid minion of Wall Street.:

...it was not the policy of the Fed to prick bubbles by monetary means [i.e., by raising interest rates].

His speech gave Wall Street the go-ahead it was looking for, the confirmation that the stock market bubble was not going to be stopped "prematurely" by the Fed; that hundreds of billions of dollars now lay ahead for the investment banks in yet-to-be collected profits—no matter what the consequences for the markets or America.

Now allowed to grow unimpeded by Washington, DC, the stock market bubble would grow unabated until its collapse three years later in March 2000, the collapse of the largest speculative bubble in history.

Do you remember what happened in the aftermath of that collapse? What the US had to do to keep the US from slipping into a deflationary cycle and potentially another Great Depression?

- Fearful the collapse of Japanese and US stock market bubbles would rekindle deflationary pressures, Central Banks in the US and Japan slashed interest rates to historically low levels in order to stimulate demand.

- The combined US and Japanese low interest rates caused prices of real estate, stocks, and bonds in world markets to suddenly inflate as buyers now had access to very cheap credit.

- These low interest rates fueled a rise in demand resulting in higher prices for real estate and global financial instruments. This sudden availability of low-interest money rekindled global inflationary pressures.

- Inflationary pressures forced Central Banks in the US, Japan, and Europe to raise interest rates.

- High interest rates caused prices of real estate and world financial markets to collapse.

- Collapsing prices will in turn once again renew downward deflationary pressures.

Hopefully, these words now have more meaning than when you first began reading this analysis. Keep reading and keep hoping, for although prayer is indeed called for, there is still hope—though there is not much time.

When Greenspan capitulated to Wall Street in the spring of 1997, his capitulation was complete. From 1997 on, his utterances became less truthful and more reflective of his new role as hand-servant of Wall Street, the complicit maestro of crowd control for the boys in the balcony.

Green-spin became more and more prevalent as time after time the good doctor would excuse some new aberration of Wall Street's dangerous greed, explaining for example that the growth of unregulated hedge funds and derivative swaps play an important role in the management of risk in today's complex markets—that any bubble is difficult to see except in hindsight and although there appeared to be a bit of "froth" in local real estate markets, Greenspan could see no bubble in US real estate prices.

In his final years as head of the Fed, Greenspan played his role well and it worked—for the boys on Wall Street. Like Dr. Nick, the pill doctor who fatally prescribed Elvis Presley all the prescription drugs he wanted, the good doctor Greenspan gave Wall Street all the low cost credit it could use—even if it was to come at the cost of America's economic health.

ALAN GREENSPAN KBE
MAESTRO NOT OF THE MARKET
BUT THOSE WHO PLAYED IT

2012 UPDATE: What Alan Greenspan lacked in understanding and foresight, he balanced with great timing. From 1987 to 2006, he presided over the greatest burst of credit-creation in history and was knighted for his apparent success. In 2006, Greenspan resigned just before his massive property bubble collapsed. The collapse of his property bubble in 2008/2009 undid everything and more Greenspan's historic credit bubble had achieved.

Section I

SECTION II

GOLD, WHY GOLD, AND WHY NOW?

Topic 7

In the absence of the gold standard, there is no way to protect savings from confiscation through inflation. There is no safe store of value.
- Alan Greenspan 1966

Gold today is valued primarily as an inflation hedge. That is so because when inflation took hold in the 1970s, gold exploded upwards, rising from $35 per ounce in 1972 to $850 per ounce in 1980, an increase of 2,428 % in just eight years.

Gold's meteoric rise dwarfed even the historic bull run of the Dow from its low of 777 in 1982 to its high of 11,723 in 2000, a comparative rise of 1,510 % that took eighteen years to accomplish. It is little wonder gold is now primarily remembered as an inflation hedge by most.

What is equally as important, however, is what happened to gold during the Great Depression, the period when deflation stopped the US and world economy dead in its tracks after the collapse of the historic 1929 stock market bubble, then the largest collapse of a speculative bubble in history.

During the Great Depression, the stock market lost 90 % of its value. If, in 1928, $100,000 had been invested in the Dow, in 1938 the investment would have been worth only $10,000. If, however, that $100,000 had been invested in gold mining stocks, the investment would have increased to $1,000,000 by 1938. Gold is a hedge against inflation and deflation.

GOLD IS A HEDGE AGAINST MONETARY CHAOS

That gold is important in times of inflation or deflation begs the point of why gold is so important now. Inflation may very well be the ultimate destroyer of financial wealth in the future. Or perhaps deflation will be the means by which current imbalances are destructively resolved. In either case, gold would be the ideal haven in both instances.

It is in this interim period, though, before the "rupture", as it were, that gold also has a unique place and value. Here, its value is not as a hedge against inflation or deflation; its attraction lies in its most fundamental role as a storehouse of value.

The "value" of money lies solely in its perception as a safe-store of present value. When this is questioned, the value of money itself becomes suspect; and, because currencies are no longer linked to gold, the value of paper money is being questioned as never before.

> *The dollar has been subjected to a great amount of exchange-rate volatility, and it's not a good store of value anymore.*
> -Joseph Stiglitz, January 2007, Nobel Laureate
> Professor of Economics, Columbia University

The questioning of money as a storehouse of value was set in motion by the US de-linking the US dollar from gold. Not only was the world reserve currency no longer convertible to gold or silver, the constraints upon the overall supply of currency no longer existed.

According to the Bretton-Woods agreement, the amount of US dollars was restricted to the amount of gold possessed by the US. The more gold, the more US dollars could be in circulation; the less gold, the less dollars.

When the US de-linked the US dollar from gold, this constraint no longer existed and what next happened changed the value of money forever—the creation of massive amounts of paper money first from the US and later from Japan began in earnest.

Paper money is now flooding the world and the world is literally choking on it. When money is valuable it is somewhat scarce; then it is saved, kept as a storehouse of value until a use for it is found.

Today, there is so much paper money in circulation, the very value of money is diminished, and, as a result, gold is now seen as a more preferable storehouse of value. This is what is now driving the price of gold upwards in world markets.

Because of the easy availability of paper money in the US, global trade imbalances are at all-time highs. When transfers of gold were necessary to balance trade deficits, such continuing and large imbalances were impossible. Now commonplace and growing, they are threatening the stability of the world economy.

Ben Bernanke, current head of the US Federal Reserve Bank, has blamed the constantly growing US trade imbalance on Asia's high savings rate. Like an alcoholic blaming the corner drugstore's liquor sale for his failing liver, there is little truth to Bernanke's words. What is true, however, is this:

THERE IS NOTHING MORE DANGEROUS
THAN WHEN A NATION LIES TO ITSELF

Calculated misdirection, i.e., crowd control, however, does buy Bernanke and the US time, and time to the US is becoming as scarce as credit-money is not. Time is running out for the US; and, as it runs out for the US, it's running out for you too.

IN A RUNAWAY INFLATION CASH IS WORTHLESS
IN A DEFLATIONARY DEPRESSION CASH IS KING
DURING BOTH GOLD WILL BE PRICELESS

We are living in times never before seen or experienced. You now understand that something as basic as money is not what it once was; that the US and the US dollar no longer are what they appear to be. You understand that much of what you believed was true is not and that what you believed could not be true, in fact, is.

DO NOT LOOK TO THE GOVERNMENT FOR HELP

Topic 8

There is one safeguard known generally to the wise, which is an advantage and security to all, but especially to democracies as against despots. What is it? Distrust.

- Demosthenes

It is my recommendation that you view the US government much as the residents of New Orleans should have viewed the US government prior to, during, and after Hurricane Katrina. This is unfortunate; but, unfortunately, it is also true.

The US government no more intends to save you from the financial ruin that awaits the nation than it intended to save the citizens of New Orleans from the ravages of Hurricane Katrina. And much as the government denied knowing beforehand the danger Hurricane Katrina posed, the US government will likewise deny the dangers you now face because of America's deteriorating financial condition.

Crowd control, not the truth, is what you will hear. To believe otherwise because you want to believe will be your undoing.

Although the correction in the nation's homebuilding will continue, it won't be enough to stunt a strong US economy. A slowing housing industry may even help curb inflation.
-Susan Bies, Federal Reserve System Governor, January 2007

The greatest resource of Americans has been their independence and resilience. It will be so again in the future. Depend on that, on yourself, on your friends and family, not the crafted words of the President or his spokesperson. Their intent is only to help themselves—and trust me on this—to the best of their ability they have already done so.

Those in government will deny this, saying that the very purpose of a democratic government is to look out for the welfare of the people and, indeed, so it is. It is, however, not their purpose. Their purpose has been to look out for themselves and they have done so on a grand scale.

You, not the government, are your greatest resource in these times; that, and your faith if you have any. And if you don't, hear me on this—better get some now while the getting's still good.

PRICELESS INVESTMENT ADVICE
SELL WHAT IS GOING DOWN
BUY WHAT IS GOING UP

Topic 9

Now you know why I buy more gold and silver every time they drop in value in the current economic environment. What smart investor wouldn't gladly spend funny money to buy real money?
- Robert Kiyosaki, author of Rich Dad, Poor Dad

Imagine your investment opportunities as a grand smorgasbord. While the prime rib roast certainly looks good, you've been told by someone in the kitchen it's old. So forget it and look for something more to your liking. Maybe in an hour or so a new and better cut will be brought out, so wait and come back then.

Such should be your approach to investments; much is offered but it helps to have someone in the kitchen who knows better than you what's good, what's bad, and what's the daily special.

In the appendix (addendum I), you will find my gold list of recommended advisors that will help you through these dangerous times. To them, what has been explained and revealed in the preceding pages is nothing new, and if there was a detail of which they were as yet unaware, it nonetheless fits with what they already understand, with their view of where we are and where we are headed.

Some of them believe this will all end in rampant inflation, some believe a deflationary depression will once again resolve the monetary mistakes of the past, many are still undecided. All, however, agree that we have gone too far to return safely, that so many critical mistakes have been made the system can no longer be fixed, a change of oil will not undo the damage that has been done. Perhaps a completely new vehicle will be called for.

Those who know what to do, however, do suggest you now choose a different menu of investments than what you have been used to. Old methods of investing will no longer work. An investment that was once conservative and cautious may now be a certain path to loss. And a known but untried strategy may be the very vehicle that will bring returns many times your original investment.

The menu of investment options will be different for each of you. Those who enjoy investing on your own will choose to follow advice that will help advise you what to do. Those who prefer having their assets managed by another will be able to do so for there are trustworthy money managers that can steer your assets away from potential losses towards safer and more profitable areas of investment in these uncertain times.

In the past, keeping cash in savings accounts, in CDs, or money market funds was considered safe. Today, that is no longer so. In a time when currencies may lose 20 % to 50 % of its value, holding currencies is nothing but a losing proposition, except perhaps temporarily. Perhaps it was prudent and wise in the past but not anymore. The times they are a 'changin' and quickly so.

THE CUSP OF THE RUPTURE
THE BEGINNING OF THE END

Topic 10

It's like Peter Pan who shouts, "Do you believe?" And the crowd shouts back, in unison, "We believe". You can believe in fairy tales and Peter Pan as long as the crowd shouts back, "we believe". That's what the dollar represents, a store of value that people believe in. They can keep on believing, but there comes a point that they don't.
                                    - Bill Gross, BusinessWeek interview June 2006

The peaking of the US housing bubble and world financial markets marked a critical turning point towards the financial tsunami now awaiting us. The process itself will take months, possibly even years, but perhaps not even that.

The world economy has entered a new and dangerous phase; it is now on its way down; and, while there will be a few rebounds along the way, the downward course has been inexorably set. This is the third and final leg of what began in the 1950s. It will end with the Time Of The Vulture.

An apt metaphor for this process is the progression of a fatal disease which we will call "economic-collapse". The first stage of economic-collapse was from 1950 to 1971 when the illness began.

Policies were then set in motion that would lead to the loss of America's gold. This could be characterized as the "silent stage" of the disease because no one knew the consequences of what was happening, let alone what was happening itself. The country was unaware of the actions and policies of what President Eisenhower called "the military-industrial complex"; policies that were to erode and destroy the economic foundation of America.

Indeed, even those in the military-industrial complex did not know this. They believed they were pursuing goals that were in the best interests of America. Instead, they had made a fatal error in judgment that was to affect us all—a judgment that was to ultimately undermine the financial well-being and future of the entire nation.

The second stage of economic-collapse was not invisible as was the first. Here, the consequences of what had been set in motion in the first stage became apparent. America's gold was all but gone and this fact could no longer be hidden.

In 1971, the US announced it would no longer convert US dollars to gold and, in 1973, the end of the relationship between gold and the world reserve currency was officially announced. The consequences of this have been world-changing and the chickens are only now coming home to roost.

No longer needing to balance its trade deficit with accompanying transfers of gold, the US trade imbalance then began to increase rapidly. The last US trade surplus occurred soon thereafter, in 1975, a surplus of $12.4 billion. That was the last time it was to happen.

In 2005 the US trade deficit reached $725.8 billion, fully 6.2 % of the US GDP (gross domestic product). It is estimated the 2006 US trade deficit may reach $975 billion, almost 7 % of the US GDP. A negative trade balance of 5 % GDP is the level historically associated with a currency crisis. Do not think for a moment money managers around the world are unaware of these figures and the implications for the US dollar.

During this second stage of economic-collapse, another result of the US de-linking the dollar from gold occurred. No longer needing to restrict its money supply to the amount of gold it possessed, the US money supply began to multiply rapidly, and in conjunction with supply-side adjustments to the US tax code, the longest bull market in the history of capitalism began.

In truth, it was the beginning of an extraordinary speculative bubble that was to end with the dot.com collapse in 2000. In 1982, with the Dow at 777, US equities began a spectacular ascent culminating eighteen years later with the Dow at 11,723 in March 2000.

From 1995 to 1999, however, M3, the US broad money supply, was rapidly growing by 32 % annually. And, in 2001, after the US stock markets had collapsed, the US money supply increased even more, M3 growing by 50 %, from $600 billion in 2000 to $1.1 trillion in 2001. The historic rise in the Dow turned out to be nothing more than a financial bubble driven by excessive monetary expansion.

This unprecedented growth in US dollars not only created financial bubbles in the US, but in worldwide markets as well. In his book, *The Dollar Crisis*, former World Bank analyst Richard Duncan draws a direct connection between large positive trade balances with the US and resultant bubbles and domestic economic crises for its trading partners—Japan in 1980s, Thailand in 1990s, etc.

Japan was the first victim of a large positive balance of trade with the US. Under Bretton-Woods, trade imbalances had to be counterbalanced by transfers of gold, therefore large and continuing trade imbalances did not exist as they were impossible to sustain.

Gold, then, was the barrier through which currencies had to pass before they could enter another nation's currency realm. The barrier, though invisible at the time, prevented any excessive buildup of foreign currencies such as now regularly occurs with the US dollar.

Like nature protecting the fetus with a placental barrier, direct transfers of gold or a reserve currency convertible to gold protected domestic economies from the fiscally irresponsible actions of their neighbors or trading partners. Inflation could be controlled locally.

After 1973, when the world reserve currency, the US dollar, was no longer convertible to gold, this protective barrier ceased to exist and with it the protection it afforded. As a consequence, after 1973 the unrestrained inflationary policies of the US began to "infect" the domestic economies of its trading partners; and when a trade imbalance with the US occurred, so did the effects of the accompanying monetary infection.

The first almost-fatal victim of this was to be Japan in the 1980s. The flood of US dollars helped cause the collapse of the Japanese Nikkei in 1989 and pushed Japan into a deflationary cycle from which it has not emerged; and unless China more successfully seals off its domestic economy than did Japan, China runs the very real risk of succeeding Japan as another victim of a burgeoning "successful" balance of trade with America.

Because the collapse of the Nikkei plunged the Japanese economy into a downward deflationary cycle, Japan in 1999 slashed interest rates to an unheard of 0 % in order to prevent a further descent into a deflationary depression; and, it was this availability of 0 % money that gave rise to the now infamous yen-carry trade.

The availability of "free" money from Japan led international investment bankers to borrow as much as they could in order to speculate in financial markets all over the world; and the consequences of fueling a worldwide credit-driven boom in equities will soon be felt during the coming third and final stage of economic collapse.

This flood of "free" money in the form of 0 % yen had the same effect as giving free lap dance tickets to all the male patrons in the bar. The lap dance rooms were then flooded with patrons flush with cash and the cost of tipping the dancers went through the roof.

However, the behavior of the bar patrons, e.g. international investment bankers, in the lap dance rooms is now a significant factor in the growing instability of world markets. Anxiously and desperately competing with each other for the attention of the dancers, today's investment bankers have literally bet the bank in the search for higher yields.

The days of yesterday's banker are long gone, when qualification for a home loan was not a sure thing, when bankers would look at prospective buyers with a dubious cynicism doubtful that what was written on the mortgage application was true.

That mortgage banker is gone, gone with the times that produced him. Today's banker is more likely to be found at the crap tables in today's financial bourses, NASDAQ, COMEX, the NYSE, TOCOM, the London Bourse, elbowing their way to the table loaded with borrowed money to place leveraged bets on the riskiest investments in the search for the highest returns.

2012 UPDATE: The leveraged bets of investment bankers started going bad in 2007 and in 2008. Wall Street banks, Bear Stearns and Lehman Bros, collapsed along with AIG, the world's largest insurance company which had to be rescued by the US government in order to survive.

Because of fraudulent accounting practices now allowed by the SEC, most large banks appear to be solvent. They are not. The government support of large banks is necessary for the benefit of both. Without banks, governments could not borrow the massive sums they need and without governments, the bankers' paper banknotes could not pass as real money.

> The bankers' three-hundred year ponzi-scheme of credit and debt is coming to an end; and when the dust settles, both banks and governments will have fallen. The process has begun.

WHEN BANKERS BECOME GAMBLERS AND FISHERMEN PREY WIDOWS AND ORPHANS IT'S NOT YOUR DAY

Topic 11

...circumstances seem to me as dangerous and intractable as any I can remember.
                        - Paul Volker, former US Fed Chairman, 2005

When all is said and done, when the economic-collapse has come and gone, when the time of the vulture is past, economists will discuss what went so terribly wrong and questions such as, "could it have been averted?" will be asked. At that time, it is likely the name Hyman Minsky will surface and his theories examined in the light of what transpired. And, I think, the consensus might well be that Hyman Minsky had his finger on it all along.

IS THERE A HYMAN IN GREENSPAN'S FUTURE?

The above question ran as a constant subtext to Greenspan's reassurance of the markets that although there was some concern, that fundamentally all was well and would continue to be so.

If the maestro of crowd control had ever read Hyman Minsky—and he probably did, for Greenspan is as knowledgeable as he is ambitious, he knew best to keep that knowledge to himself; for his masters on Wall Street, above all, would not appreciate his warning the chickens that the gate was not secure and that predators were about.

Hyman Minsky observed that as capital markets matured, they

changed; and, as they changed, they became increasingly unstable; that speculative bubbles and steep declines would increase in size and intensity and riskier investments would inevitably replace those which had been safe.

And, indeed, that does appear to be the case, as we lurch from bubble to bubble in the desperate hope that the next bubble will bail us out of the last—**but if this bubble is indeed the last, we are not going to be bailed out again.**

As we enter this third stage of economic-collapse, what is now occurring is the result of what has gone before; and with Minsky in mind, perhaps nothing is as responsible as the Federal Reserve Bank and our fractional banking system. What is generally not understood is that our entire system of money is built not on savings, but on debt.

Money as we know it is but debt in paper form. If all obligations of the Federal Reserve Bank were to be paid in full, money as we know it would disappear at the very same instant.

We all know how much money is around and its supply is growing rapidly; and as the supply of money grows, so does the amount of debt. Trillions have now replaced billions in our vocabulary. Bazillions might well be next and bababazillions after that—except there will be no next time.

OUR MONEY SYSTEM IS BUILT ON DEBT
AND OUR CONTINUED "PROSPERITY" IS PREDICATED
ON THE CONTINUAL GROWTH OF THAT DEBT
AS MORE MONEY, I.E. DEBT, IS CONSTANTLY
NEEDED TO SERVICE OLD DEBT

The Federal Reserve interest rate which the world financial community watches with so much obsessive interest is the rate the Federal Reserve Bank charges for the creation of new debt, i.e. new money. The lower the interest rate, the more debt/money is created. The higher the interest rate, the less debt/money created.

THE WORLD ECONOMY IS NOW ADDICTED TO A
CONSTANT AND INCREASING FLOW OF DEBT

A CONSTANT AND INCREASING FLOW OF DEBT
LEADS TO A CONSTANT INCREASE
IN THE RATE OF INFLATION

A CONSTANT AND INCREASING FLOW OF DEBT IS
NECESSARY TO SERVICE ALREADY-INCURRED DEBT

IF THE FLOW OF DEBT RAPIDLY INCREASES,
RUNAWAY INFLATION WILL RESULT

A CONSTANTLY-INCREASING FLOW OF DEBT LEADS
TO AN ACCUMULATION OF DEBT AT A RATE
THAT PRODUCTIVITY AND SAVINGS CAN
NO LONGER SERVICE

IF THE FLOW OF DEBT REMAINS CONSTANT OR
DECREASES A RECESSION WILL RESULT

IF THE DEMAND FOR DEBT CONTINUALLY DECREASES
A DEFLATIONARY DEPRESSION WILL RESULT WITH
MASSIVE DEFAULTS OF MONETARY OBLIGATIONS

The critical understanding is this:

THE PRESENT DEBT-BASED MONEY SYSTEM IS
INHERENTLY DESTRUCTIVE TO PRODUCTIVITY
AND SAVINGS.

THE CURRENT DEFINITION OF PRODUCTIVITY IS AS
FLAWED AND DESTRUCTIVE AS THE SYSTEM
IT REPRESENTS.

PRODUCTIVITY CANNOT BE MEASURED BY ITS COST,
ONLY ITS COST IS SO MEASURED.

The true cost of a "financial-services" economy is the ultimate destruction of true productivity and savings. It is no coincidence that the US, with the largest financial service sector in the world, now has a negative rate of savings.

The Federal Reserve Bank was created by an act of Congress in 1913, almost one hundred years ago. One hundred years is more than enough time to determine if an experiment has worked. Only recently, the YES side seemed to be winning. Now, the NO side is catching up and is beginning to pull away.

LADIES AND GENTLEMEN
PLACE YOUR BETS
THE LAST ROUND IS ABOUT TO BEGIN

Topic 12

Betting is always risky. But now, doing nothing, is the riskiest bet of all.

The third stage of economic-collapse is now underway. If you do not want to be a victim of what is to be a financial tsunami, you must take steps to prevent it. And this, the beginning of the third stage, is the last time you will be able to do so.

But if you do take the right steps, if you do choose the right investment strategies, you will profit as perhaps never before.

It is never easy to understand or accept anything that does not conform to previously-held beliefs. The human mind accepts only that which confirms what it already "knows"—this is true whether you are a Muslim, a Buddhist, a Christian, or an atheist.

If you believe the US is financially healthy, that with hard work and a little luck you will do fine in the days ahead, then what has been presented here is directly at odds with what you "know".

And, as such, your mind is predisposed to reject the conclusions and premises of this book. To do so, however, will put your future and the future of those entrusted to your care at extreme risk.

Trust is a critically important issue now and we have been told since birth to trust those in control. Unfortunately, we are told this because our trust makes their control so much easier; not because their trust is deserved or justified.

It is now time for you to decide what and whom to trust. Your very future depends on it. God and your intuition is a good place to start.

You now know the US dollar is at risk in the world markets, that with the largest deficit of any nation in history, with the largest trade imbalance of any nation in history, with the largest debt of any nation in history, the outlook for the US is not promising.

This is obviously not the party line of those in control, those in government who know what is true, who know what is actually happening and what is actually at risk in the days ahead. This is the same government that was warned the levees could be breached by Hurricane Katrina and said nothing to the citizens of New Orleans or the nation.

This is the same government that is now reassuring you, its citizens, that all is well; while ensuring that the rich and their friends will have more than enough to survive the tough times ahead. And if you still believe the US government is "your" government, be aware that you now do so at your own risk.

Imagine the US to be a ship, the USS US as it were. The captain of the ship, the President, elected by those on board, appears to be in charge. But that's only how it appears. President Eisenhower's reluctance to challenge the owners, the military-industrial complex, is evidence that this is not so. It is the ship's owners and their financiers on Wall Street who have the real power, not the captain.

The US government has been captive to these powerful financial interests for decades. If Americans attempt to buy discounted prescription drugs from Canada, they are threatened by the government they elected to protect them.

If US ranchers want to test their cattle for mad-cow disease, they can be prosecuted by the US government for so doing. Today, US regulatory agencies are more agents for those they are charged to regulate than they are overseers of the public good.

When the dot.com bubble was allowed to grow until it collapsed, it was because the ship's owners pressured the ship's navigator, Alan Greenspan, to continue on course even though Greenspan warned that an extremely large iceberg was directly ahead.

To the owners, billions in profits were more important than either the ship's safety or the well-being of its passengers. Greenspan was right and the USS US soon collided with the iceberg, causing the largest speculative bubble in history to collapse and the rest is history—well not all of it yet.

While the USS US is taking on water and listing badly, you are reading this hoping that you can somehow save yourself and your loved ones from the disaster that appears to await you and your fellow passengers.

The passengers, although they've been reassured by the ship's captain that all is well, there is nothing to worry about and we'll get through this patch of rough weather in no time, are beginning to worry.

They realized that the ship's captain, President George W. Bush, the son of a previous captain, isn't quite up to the job and there's even grumbling among those who elected him that this might be so [note: Barack Obama's economic advisors are essentially the same as those that advised Bush, i.e. Wall Street lobbyists and bankers. Economically, expect more of the same, albeit with a more liberal political "twist".]

But the ship's owners think he's doing just fine. After all, although the passengers elected him, he works for them. And although the shipping line is now heavily indebted and going broke, the captain has allowed the owners to take their money off the top. And while the ship may be going down, the fortunes of those in the first class cabins have never been better.

Today, these powerful interest groups, the military-industrial complex and Wall Street bankers, control both US domestic and foreign policies. The decision to go to war is perhaps the most momentous decision a nation can make—and Americans, the passengers of the USS US, were deceived from the very beginning about the reasons for doing so.

The war had nothing to do with weapons of mass destruction. That was a selling point, a salesman's phony and now fatal excuse to sell a war to a frightened nation. The war was also never about spreading democracy. That was an afterthought. The Iraq war was really about oil, money, and rearranging geopolitical boundaries in the Middle East. But that wouldn't sell on Fox News so they made up reasons that would.

The blunder now called the war in Iraq was conceived and instigated in the office of former Vice-President Dick Cheney prior to 9/11. And, Cheney, the former CEO of Halliburton Corporation made sure Halliburton would do quite well when the invasion took place— for Dick Cheney and Halliburton are part and parcel of the military-industrial complex, those responsible for the disappearance of America's gold, its priceless freedoms, and the consequent problems we now face.

> *There exists a shadowy Government with its own Air Force, its own Navy, its own fundraising mechanism, and the ability to pursue its own ideas of national interest, free from all checks and balances, and free from the law itself.*
> - US Senator Daniel K. Inouye, Senate Iran-Contra Hearings

Before the US invaded Iraq in 2003, Halliburton was 19th on the U.S. Army's list of contractors. After the invasion, Halliburton became the Army's number one contractor, charging the US $4.2 billion for its services. In 2005, Halliburton billed the US in excess of $7 billion. In 2006, Halliburton expected to receive at least $4 billion more from the US government.

In war, there are winners and losers. The US may be doing badly in Iraq along with the Iraqis, but the same can't be said for Halliburton and the many private Pentagon contractors. Pentagon accountants have stated they are uncertain as to why Halliburton's KBR unit billed the government for $1.8 billion for work that was apparently never undertaken or completed.

THE ANSWER IS OBVIOUS:
BECAUSE THEY COULD

When Cheney was CEO of Halliburton, Halliburton's tax payments went from $302 million in 1998 to zero in 1999, a year in which Halliburton also received an $85 million refund from the IRS. During his first five years as Vice-President, Cheney's stock options in Halliburton increased in value 3,281 %, from $241,498 to over $8 million.

With Cheney as Vice-President of the US, Halliburton was awarded billions of dollars in no-bid US government contracts for supplying food and oil in Iraq and for reconstruction work in the aftermath of Hurricane Katrina.

Worse than traitors in arms are the men who pretend loyalty to the flag, [and] feast and fatten on the misfortunes of the Nation.
- Abraham Lincoln

To the owners of the USS US and their bankers, this is a win-win situation. To the passengers, it is a losing proposition. The difference is that the passengers don't get a vote except on Election Day, and that vote means absolutely nothing.

Cheney has said as Vice-President that his money is held in a blind trust; and indeed it is, for without the blindness and trust of Americans the US would never have fallen into his grasp and others like him. In the 1950s, the US was the most powerful nation in the world, admired for its freedoms and leadership; but now, only a half century later, the US is but a pauper on paper, its freedoms a fading memory of a once magnificent past and its currency a soon-to-be-greatly-discounted piece of paper on the world's foreign exchange markets.

Blind trust is almost always paid for with blood and money. This time is no different. What you know about your government is what your government has wanted you to know. You believed them in the past and look at what is happening now. Believe them in the future and you will find you will have no future at all. The choice, as always, is yours.

When the USS US starts to sink, most Americans will dutifully line up on deck as instructed by the ship's officers, told that lifeboats will soon be lowered for them to board. What they will discover is that the lifeboats are already full with passengers from the upper decks, from the first class cabins, the corporate and presidential suites.

The passengers from the lower decks and steerage will be, as always, left to fend for themselves, hoping against hope that their WalMart life vests will protect them and their families from the frigid economic waters that will soon surround them.

Personally, if you're still reading this while the USS US is still afloat, I suggest you'd better start looking for something that might actually float.

2012 UPDATE: The collapse I predicted in *How to Survive the Crisis and Prosper in the Process* began shortly after I presented my analysis to the Positive Deviant Network in 2007. In 2008, the severity of the economic collapse was so severe; Americans overwhelmingly voted out the Republicans and elected a Democrat, Barack Obama.

Barack Obama was elected on a platform of change. Like most politicians, however, he did not deliver what he promised. This is because the Democratic Party now answers to the same moneyed elite that traditionally fueled the Republican Party.

Do not expect substantive change to come from either the Democrats or Republicans. Corporate money now controls each political party and although the differences in social agendas are as wide as ever, social issues are just a device used by the ruling elites to divide Americans while they steal the country blind.

My advice is the same as when the book was written. Trust neither political party to do what's in the best interests of the nation. Today, surviving the crisis is your most important goal and the less you expect politicians to help you, the better off you will be.

Section II

SECTION III

THE US GOVERNMENT
THE US DOLLAR AND GOLD

Topic 13

Although the gold standard could hardly be portrayed as having produced a period of price tranquility, it was the case that the price level in 1929 was not much different, on net, from what it had been in 1800. But, in the two decades following the abandonment of the gold standard in 1933, the consumer price index in the United States nearly doubled. And, in the four decades after that, prices quintupled.

- Alan Greenspan

In 1973, when the US officially de-linked the dollar from gold, it was less a final divorce than a continuing separation. The US dollar, unlike gold, had been defined by its relationship with gold at $35 per ounce; and when the official relationship ended, the US dollar was on its own. Gold, however, has been deeply affected by the US dollar ever since and any investment in gold must take into account the continuing relationship between the two.

Because the US dollar was no longer backed by gold, the dollar's value now depended upon investor perception, and the US did not want a foot race to develop between the dollar and gold as to which was a better storehouse of value. In such a race, gold, not paper money, would be the easy victor.

The US government had to do something and so it did. It decided to force the price of gold lower so investors would favor paper over gold. Not only did this new policy make sense to the US government, it would ultimately make Wall Street a whole lot of money.

The US government began to manipulate the price of gold soon after officially announcing that the US dollar was no longer convertible. Because all currencies were no longer tied to gold via the US dollar, all paper currencies were potentially vulnerable to any rise in gold's

49

price. And, because of this, Central Bankers around the world were forced to collude with the US to collectively suppress its value. Central Bankers would call this process "managing gold".

The US government's first act to "manage" gold took place in December 1974 when it announced it would be selling two million ounces of gold. The price of gold, which had begun to rise after being de-linked from the US dollar, fell on the news that a large supply was soon to be available. This was exactly what the US government wanted.

Next, in 1975 the International Monetary Fund, which has often functioned as an extension of the US, announced it would sell an additional 25 million ounces of its gold. These two announcements alone would have been more than enough to drive the price of gold significantly lower except for one not-insignificant detail—at the exact same time, US inflation rates began spiraling out of control.

From 1976 to 1980, US inflation increased from 5.22 % to 13.91 % and the price of gold responded accordingly; skyrocketing from $102 per ounce in 1976 to $850 in 1980. Instead of forcing gold down, the market absorbed all the gold the US and IMF sold and then some. This is a lesson that bears remembering because gold will soon again experience a meteoric rise in spite of government attempts to the contrary.

After inflation was brought under control with interest rates as high as 21.5 %, the price of gold dropped in 1981. And, for the next twenty years, Central Banks in collusion with large investment banks successfully prejudiced investors against gold in favor of paper currencies. There was money to be made in bull markets built on credit and debt, and money flowed freely towards paper assets and away from gold.

But in 2000 with the collapse of the NASDAQ dot.com bubble, suddenly the financial edifice of debt and credit no longer looked so good and the price of gold began to move upwards. At the same time Central Banks were flooding financial markets with liquidity in the form of cheap credit, creating a property bubble in the US and high asset prices in global financial markets.

But the liquidity driven surge from 2001 to 2004 that had lifted gold along with stocks and other commodities to market highs collapsed in mid-May 2006. The reason for the collapse is that Japan had been withdrawing liquidity from the market for months in an attempt to slow down the dangerous growth of its money supply.

Although by May 2006 the Japanese had yet to raise interest rates (they did so in July with a 0.25 % raise), the Japanese had been withdrawing liquidity from its banking system since early 2005. Prior to the mid-May top, the Japanese Central Bank had withdrawn a total of $140 billion in deposits from Japanese banks over the previous 14 months.

In a fractional reserve banking system with a 10:1 loan to deposit ratio, deposits of $140 billion dollars create $1,400,000,000,000 in loans. The withdrawal of $140 billion in deposits meant the Japanese withdrew $1.4 trillion of liquidity from the markets during the previous year.

That withdrawal of liquidity signaled to investment bankers that the yen-carry trade was perhaps coming to an end, that cheap money was to be a thing of the past and it was now time to take some winnings off the table. But when they all tried to collect their winnings at the same time, the prices of stocks and commodities fell as one.

This signaled the beginning of the end, the resolution of past sins of Central Bank monetary policies, the painful correction that always follows excess much as withdrawal follows addiction. Except in this case, the party has been going on for years and was paid for with credit, not hard cash. And because hard cash disappeared in 1971 with the end of the convertibility of the US dollar, in the end gold will be the designated payment of choice, not paper.

2012 UPDATE: The economic crisis has brought gold to the attention of the previously unknowing and unaware; and, although most are still unknowing and unaware, the US government is more focused than ever in keeping it this way.

> When the crisis reaches a certain stage, Western bankers whose past power depended on the stability of their paper assets will lose control of the price of gold. It hasn't happened yet but, someday, it will; and that day is coming sooner rather than later.

CAUSE AND CONSEQUENCE
THE JAPANESE BUBBLE AND DEFLATION
A BANKER'S NIGHTMARE

Topic 14

There is no means of avoiding the final collapse of a boom brought about by credit (debt) expansion. The alternative is only whether the crisis should come sooner as the result of a voluntary abandonment of further credit (debt) expansion, or later as a final and total catastrophe of the currency system involved.

- Ludwig von Mises

In 1996, when Fed Chairman Alan Greenspan warned America about the dangers of irrational exuberance in the stock markets, he was warning that what had just happened in Japan could happen in America.

Deflation, the dreaded nightmare of Central Bankers—an increasing cycle of decreasing demand—had reappeared in Japan after the collapse of its stock market in 1990. And, in March 2000, just as Greenspan had predicted, the US stock markets collapsed and set in motion the deflationary forces that Greenspan and Central Bankers feared.

Deflation's last appearance in the US had been during the Great Depression when it brought the US and world economies to a grinding halt after the collapse of the US 1929 stock market bubble. Now, the collapse of an even larger 2000 dot.com bubble was again threatening the financial well-being of the world.

If Japan and the US, the world's largest two economies, were slowing due to deflationary pressures, Europe and the rest of the world might soon follow. And, if that happened, a repeat of the 1930s Great Depression was a distinct possibility.

Because the US and Japanese Central Banks slashed interest rates to unheard-of low levels in order to increase demand, this unleashed a flood of low-cost mortgages in the US, and the availability of "free" money in Japan for investment bankers to borrow and invest in worldwide markets.

This flood of new money, i.e., new debt, soon led to a bubble in US real estate prices which caused an increase in consumer spending as homeowners rapidly drew out newly-gained equity to enjoy their newfound "wealth".

This historic flood of liquidity into the world's two largest economies did slow the deflationary forces in Japan and the US. But this flood of credit-money no more stopped deflation than giving heroin to an addict solves the addiction. It gave temporary relief but the problem remained.

RESPITE IS NOT RESOLUTION

The US real estate bubble deflated when 1 % interest rates were raised to 5.25 %. The bubble, however, is leaving in its wake a mountain of unpaid debt in the form of subprime, refinanced and adjustable rate mortgages.

The US Federal Reserve had created a real estate bubble in the attempt to mitigate the consequences of the dot.com stock bubble. What is not known, however, is that the US also had a direct hand in the Japanese stock market bubble that collapsed in 1990.

THE CHICKENS ARE COMING HOME TO ROOST

During the 1980s, the Japanese economy was booming. Its exports dominated virtually every market they entered and its balance of trade with the US (unfettered by the need to transfer gold) was the largest in history. As a consequence, paper money was flowing into Japan at an unprecedented rate. Prices were beginning to move upwards and new money was flowing into the stock market at an unprecedented rate, causing the Nikkei to rise faster than market fundamentals might dictate.

By the mid-1980s, the Japanese Central Bank decided to slow the economy down by raising interest rates. This action would dampen any inflationary tendencies and prevent a stock market bubble from forming. However, as logical as this solution was, it was to be opposed by the US government and never implemented.

At the time, most of the Japanese money was being invested in US Treasuries, as the Reagan administration was borrowing heavily to fund its military buildup. During Reagan's presidency, US government debt tripled from one to four trillion dollars, the greatest percentage increase of US debt in history.

The US knew that any rise in Japanese interest rates would slow the flow of Japanese funds to the US. Japanese investors would much prefer to keep their money in Japan if interest rates were high enough.

But during this time, the Reagan administration needed a constant flow of foreign dollars to pay for its military expenditures and when it heard about the plans of the Japanese Central Bank, it did more than register a protest. It threatened Japan with economic sanctions.

If the Japanese went ahead with their interest rate increase, the US threatened to retaliate with import tariffs on Japanese automobiles, electronics, and consumer goods. This threat was real enough to cause the Japanese to cancel their interest rate increase.

As a result, the US military buildup continued and the price of Japanese real estate and stocks, fueled by excessive amounts of liquidity, exploded upwards. Japanese real estate prices increased 70 times over and stock prices increased over 100-fold, with the Nikkei reaching a market top at 38,992 in January 1990.

As with all speculative bubbles, the Nikkei collapsed—and the collapse of the Nikkei in 1990 unleashed deflationary forces not seen since the Great Depression of the 1930s. Prices of stocks and real estate in Japan crashed and began a long and steep multi-year descent.

Commercial real estate lost 80 % of its value in the next decade and the Nikkei fell from 38,992 in 1990 to 8,237 in 2003. Deflationary cycles are long and protracted and if not stopped will become deflationary depressions, an economic phenomenon for which there are no ready answers.

In a deflationary cycle, prices fall because of decreasing demand for services and goods. Should deflation take root in the US, real estate prices, stock prices, and prices of services will fall for years until a bottom is eventually found. And in a depression, when a bottom is found there will be no upward bounce. The economy will merely lie inert as it did during the 1930s.

It was because of this possibility that the US in 2001 slashed interest rates in order to prevent a slide into another depression. The lowering of interest rates, however, subsequently set in motion the largest run-up in real estate prices in US history.

When interest rates rose to 5.25 %, the lesson that what goes down must come up and what goes up must come down was learned once again. And although the descent into deflation was prevented in 2001, its current descent will be all the more disturbing because when people lose their homes, it is far more devastating than when their stock portfolios drop in value.

Credit in many ways resembles heroin, the effect is quick and, to those addicted, the feeling is one of well-being. But credit, like heroin, requires ever increasing amounts to achieve the same high, and as usage increases, so do the chances of eventual collapse. This is as true for financial markets addicted to infusions of credit as it is for addicts needing more heroin.

COLLAPSE AND DESTRUCTION MAY JUST
BE A LOWER INTEREST RATE AWAY BUT
ADDICTS JUST CAN'T HELP WANTING ONE MORE HIGH

2012 UPDATE: A deflationary cycle like what appeared in Japan after 1990 is not just a possibility but is now an increasing reality for the rest of the world. Japan has never been able to successfully deal with the large amounts of defaulting debt after its stock market bubble collapsed in 1990; and, to survive, Japan has depleted its savings and now has the largest debt per GDP of any industrialized nation.

The Japanese 'lost decade' has now become two lost decades and the chances of Japan surviving a third are non-existent. For 20 years, Japan has been forced to continually borrow more and more to keep its increasingly fragile economy afloat and its export-based economy is now importing more than it exports. Today' Japan's future is as dire as it was once promising.

Despite what central bankers say or don't say, their real fear has always been a deflationary global collapse similar to what happened in the 1930s. That fear is coming true.

The US government has spent trillions hoping that temporarily increasing public demand could provide enough time for the economy to deleverage and regain velocity sufficient to maintain growth on its own. That was what Ben Bernanke hoped would happen. It didn't.

THE EMPEROR HAS NO CLOTHES
THEN WHAT'S HE WEARING?
THE ANSWER
NOTHING

Topic 15

Monetary policy, unleashed from the constraint of domestic gold convertibility, had allowed a persistent over-issuance of money. As recently as a decade ago, central bankers, having witnessed more than a half-century of chronic inflation, appeared to confirm that a fiat currency was inherently subject to excess.

- Alan Greenspan 2002

Before you invest in gold, you should understand that the gold market is not a free market. The gold market is a managed market and is therefore subject to forces not usually encountered in markets free of government interference and manipulation.

Nonetheless, because it is subject to such forces, it is the very market you want to be in. If gold were not the important monetary metal it is, the US government and Central Banks would not be actively suppressing its price. And because it is, when paper money and paper assets lose their value, gold is the one commodity you will want to own.

The ongoing US manipulation of the gold market is intended to distort what the free market price of gold would instead reveal: (1) the presence of constantly rising inflation and (2) the constantly declining value of paper money. And these two constants, rising inflation and the declining value of paper money are built-in consequences of our present fiat credit-money system.

What we call money is nothing more than "credit-in-motion", and a constantly growing supply of credit is necessary to retire previous debt and to preserve the feeling of well-being that comes with more credit (this is called "growth" or "economic expansion"). However, like any addiction, it is the desire to feel better that inevitably leads to excess.

A constantly growing supply of credit will over time fuel more inflation and cause the value of previously issued credit-money to more rapidly decline. And if there is no measure by which this can be easily determined, then no one will be the wiser and the Ponzi scheme of fiat money can continue, at least until it implodes of its own accord, as it someday must.

A true market price of gold is the one measure that would reveal the Achilles heel of this fiat currency (credit-money) system. Wikipedia's definition of "fiat currency" is most revealing:

In economics, fiat currency or fiat money is money whose purchasing power derives from a declaratory fiat or an authoritative order of the government issuing it. It is often associated with paper money unbacked by fixed assets, issued without the promise of redemption in some other form, and accepted by tradition or social convention. Fiat money is called fiduciary money in many languages.

The widespread acceptance of a fiat currency is enhanced by a central authority mandating its acceptance under penalty of law and demanding it in payment of taxes or tribute. Fiat money can be contrasted with alternative forms of currency such as commodity money and private currency.

Most currencies in the world have been fiat money since the end of the international gold standard or the Bretton-Woods system in 1971. However, some of the major currencies today, despite being based essentially on arbitrary decree, have become so trusted that they are termed hard currency.

Wikipedia's reference to "hard currency" is relevent here. Wikipedia suggests that a fiat currency can be termed a hard currency when it is trusted. A hard currency, however, is a hard currency only when it is convertible to something of value (i.e. gold) or is itself valuable. A currency is either a hard currency or a fiat currency, not one masquerading as the other.

PAPER IS PAPER
GOLD IS GOLD
ONCE THEY WERE JOINED
OR SO I'VE BEEN TOLD

However, be that as it may, Wikipedia's critical distinction regarding currencies rightly revolves around the issue of trust. That is why the US government and Central Banks manipulate gold. Gold, formerly the very foundation of paper money, is the one factor that belies the falsity of fiat currencies. Suppress gold and confidence in paper money will appear justified.

APPEARANCES ARE EVERYTHING
WELL, NOT QUITE

UNJUSTIFIED TRUST IS THE ESSENCE
OF ANY CONFIDENCE GAME

No trust, no game. Because the US spent all its gold and all currencies were anchored to gold through the dollar, all Central Bankers have been forced since the 1970s to participate in a confidence game they had not chosen of their own accord.

Now, however, that is beginning to change. In 2006 many of the world's Central Banks began to seek safer ground. Central Bankers are starting to look at gold in a new light.

The US Central Bank and its remaining allies—the coalition of the deceiving—have been ably supported in their efforts by US investment banks such as Goldman Sachs who have exploited this need for their own benefit.

This exploitation does not come without risks, however. With the price of gold rising, Goldman Sachs and other investment houses are finding themselves increasingly on the wrong side of their gold trades. The cost of bearing false witness can take many forms.

A free market price of gold would reveal that the US dollar along with all fiat currencies is, in the words of Alan Greenspan, "inherently subject to excess", constantly inflating and constantly losing value.

US Fights Inflation

And to ensure that no one knows this, to ensure that no one can see that the emperor has no clothes, the US government with all its attendant resources and power has conspired with others to distort the only measure that would allow others to see the truth.

IT IS NOT THAT WE ARE BLIND
IT IS THAT WE HAVE BEEN BLINDED

Only as the truth becomes clear will we see what needs to be done in the days ahead. We have been misled by those in power because it is in their interests for us to be so deceived. If Americans knew that their collective store of wealth, their reserves of gold, had been pillaged and sold by those in power, it would not have happened.

For a nation that is afraid to let its people judge the truth and falsehood in an open market is a nation that is afraid of its people.
> \- President John F. Kennedy

But Americans didn't know, Americans weren't told, and Americans are only now realizing that their dreams are now perhaps only dreams, that the pensions they were promised were only promised not guaranteed, that the safety nets assembled for their safety in times of need have been dismantled by those who have no need of them, that their healthcare system is but a costly trap and that tomorrow will be very different than what they had been led to expect.

Two thousand years ago the money changers were chased from the temple. It now appears they later found refuge in the US government and brought with them their fiat money system; and, in retrospect, they could not have found a more hospitable refuge in which to take both shelter and profits.

2012 UPDATE: The efforts of the US government to control the price of gold are greater today than ever. But the US is losing allies in its fight to prevent gold from becoming the investment of choice over paper assets. In 2011, for the first time in 20 years, central banks became net buyers of gold.

The large banks—HSBC, JPMorgan, Goldman Sachs, Deutsche Bank, etc.—are colluding to keep the price of gold as low as possible in order

---

to keep investors from fleeing to the safe repository of gold, paper money's barometer of systemic distress.

Nonetheless, since 2001 the price of gold has risen, a process opposed at every turn by the large banks and Western governments. Their fiefdom is faltering, however, and unless you now understand the days of banks and governments are numbered, your days will be numbered as well.

IS THAT A BALLOON?
NO THAT'S INFLATION
IS IT REALLY THAT HIGH?
NO IT'S LOWER

Topic 16

It is an ironic fact that when people are told something at variance with their actual experience, many will doubt their experience and instead believe what they have been told. And although this fact may surprise and dishearten most of us, it has the opposite effect on those in government charged with crowd control.

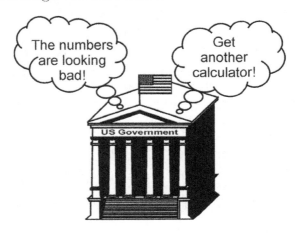

In a credit-money system, over time the constant infusion of increasing amounts of credit will inevitably lead to higher and higher rates of inflation. Because common knowledge of this fact is not in the best interests of those benefiting from the system, it is hidden away. And in the US, hiding the real rate of inflation is done the old-fashioned way, by lying about it.

Prior to the 1990s, the cost of a basket of standard goods and services was compiled. This was called the consumer price index, the CPI, and any rate of increase was considered to be the actual rate of inflation. However, in the early 1990s, this began to change.

Perhaps the old method of tracking inflation seemed outdated or quaint, much like the Geneva Accords, to Alan Greenspan and Michael Boskin, the chief economist under President Bush Sr., and a newer way of calculating the CPI was needed.

What was needed was a way that would show a slower rate of increase rather than the actual rate, a way that would save the US government money by lowering social security payments and Medicare benefits tied to the CPI, a way that would convey to global investors that all was well in America, that inflation was under control.

Irrespective of what the newly reconstituted CPI says about inflation, its effects cannot be hidden. Remember Motel 6? A low cost motel chain started in Santa Barbara, California in 1962 whose advertised price was a part of its name, $6.00 per night for accommodations.

I recently checked the prices Motel 6 charges, forty-six years later. The current room rates of Motel 6 at three different locations in Santa Barbara are:

	1966	2012	Increase
Motel 6 location #1	$6.00	$139.99	an increase of 2,333%
Motel 6 location #2	$6.00	$99.99	an increase of 1,666%
Motel 6 location #3	$6.00	$89.99	an increase of 1,499%

Marijuana also shows a similar increase in price since the 1960s.

	1966	2012	Increase
One lid of Pot	$10.00	$351.00	an increase of 3,510%

The cost of attending college at the University of Minnesota also rose.

	1966	2012	Increase
Cost per unit	$8.25	$183.00	an increase of 2,218%

THE DIFFERENCE IN PRICE BETWEEN THEN AND NOW IS DUE TO INFLATION

INFLATION IS THE INCREASING COST OF GOODS AND SERVICES CAUSED BY THE CONSTANTLY DECLINING VALUE OF PAPER MONEY OVER TIME

THE MORE MONEY YOU PRINT THE LESS IT'S WORTH

Got that? Good. It's time we understood.

M3 is the measurement of the total US money supply.

	January 1959	February 2006	Increase
M3	$292 billion	$10,276 billion	an increase of 3,419%

Note: on March 23, 2006, the US Federal Reserve Bank ceased publishing M3.

THE MORE MONEY PRINTED THE MORE EVERYTHING COSTS

In 2002, Ben Bernanke confirmed the relationship between printing money and rising prices.

...the U.S. government has a technology, called a printing press (or, today, its electronic equivalent), that allows it to produce as many U.S.

dollars as it wishes at essentially no cost. By increasing the number of U.S. dollars in circulation, or even by credibly threatening to do so, the U.S. government can also reduce the value of a dollar in terms of goods and services, which is equivalent to raising the prices in dollars of those goods and services.

Because of the continuing increase in the money supply, the dollars of today are worth less than yesterday's, and those of tomorrow will be worth less than today's. We are now, all of us, running faster and faster at unsustainable levels on a treadmill towards inevitable disaster.

These days, no one wants a tip in US dollars.
- Suzy Gershman, Born To Shop ITALY,
a Frommer's Book 2006

THE PARABLE OF AMERICANS AND INFLATION
OR
THE PARABLE OF THE FROG IN BOILING WATER

When a frog is dropped into a pot of boiling water, the frog will jump out (and live). But when a frog is dropped into a pot of cold water and the water is slowly heated to a boil, the frog will stay in the pot and boil to death.

Inflation is often discussed but its causes rarely so. This is because those who benefit from ever-increasing debt inflation would rather the chickens on the Colonel's farm remain ignorant of the true cause of their distress.

As debt-driven capital markets mature, levels of debt rise until savings disappear and productivity is destroyed. We are now at the point where the US Federal Reserve has created so much debt that the system is collapsing under its weight. But those in charge of crowd control would rather you not make the connection.

HEY, IT'S GETTING HOT IN HERE
SOMEBODY CHANGE THE THERMOMETER
YOU MEAN CHANGE THE THERMOSTAT
NO, I MEAN CHANGE THE THERMOMETER

In the June 19th   Dallas Morning News, columnist   Scott Burns pointed out the difference between opinion and actual cause regarding the inflation of the 1970s:

Many would like to blame the inflation of the 1970s on OPEC. But the reality is more complicated. When Richard Nixon ended the convertibility of the dollar into gold in 1971, oil producers had no assurance their dollars had any value.

That's where we are today, in spades.

The current indebtedness of the US now exceeds $44 trillion. In credit driven capital markets, the burden of debt becomes increasingly onerous to those unable to pay, those furthest away from the spigots of credit. To those more fortunate, to those closest to the spigots who can leverage their proximity into gain, the debt burden of others appears to be just that, someone else's problem.

But this is not so. Our denial of the collective consequence of debt is what will ultimately destroy the present economic system and the assets of all those in it.

PARABLE OF THE BIFURCATED FROG IN BOILING WATER

When a frog is dropped into a pot of boiling water, the frog will jump out and live. But if the nerves between the frog's brain and body are cut, the bifurcated frog will remain in the boiling water and die. Because its brain is disconnected from the pain of its body, the frog will not even be aware it's in danger.

The PARABLE OF THE BIFURCATED FROG IN BOILING WATER is the parable of present day America.

THOSE IN POWER ARE IN DEEP DENIAL OF WHAT THOSE LESS FORTUNATE ARE EXPERIENCING.

This is the true disconnect between those in power and those struggling to pay their bills, a disconnect that allows those in power to increase levels of credit and debt (which benefits them) until the

system implodes, **taking down everyone, both rich and poor, in
the process.**

ONLY THOSE CLOSEST TO THE
SPIGOTS OF CREDIT WILL PROFIT
AS THE OCEANS OF DOLLARS AND DEBT
EXPLODE IN SIZE
THE REST, THE MAJORITY,
NO MATTER HOW HARD THEY WORK
WILL FALL FARTHER AND FARTHER BEHIND
ULTIMATELY SUCCUMBING TO THE INCREASING
AMOUNTS OF DEBT NECESSARY TO SURVIVE
IN AN INCREASINGLY "COSTLY" WORLD

In the Bible it is written that Cain asked God, "Am I my brother's
keeper?"

The US has answered:

*No, let the free markets decide who will prosper and who will not. The
markets are the true arbiter of economic justice. Let not the hand of man
meddle in the realm of the Almighty.*

Ah, but who controls and makes the markets? The invisible hand of
Adam Smith is most certainly not the hand of the Almighty; and the
markets of today are a far cry from what they have been for
centuries.

Today, money is not produced by savings and productivity. Instead it
comes out of a spigot, the spigot of credit and debt that benefits
those closest to it. Credit and debt is what has built this temporary
edifice of prosperity. Credit and debt is what will destroy it.

Choice is the gift God gave man. We have chosen. We do not have
long to wait to see what the consequences will be.

HABERDASHERY
THE SUIT STANDARD
GOLD & BESPOKE TAILORS

Topic 17

The price of a fine suit of men's clothes can be used to show anyone who is not familiar with the price history of gold just how very cheap gold is today. With an ounce of gold, a man could buy a fine suit of clothes in the time of Shakespeare, in that of Beethoven and Jefferson, and in the Depression of the 1930's. In fact, this statement was still true in the 1980's, but not in the late 1990's. The suit standard now implies a gold price of perhaps $1,000 per troy ounce. Today, a really good man's suit can easily cost 4 ounces of gold, and that is without a vest, which once was standard.

- Forbes Magazine 1998

In 1998 when the Forbes article appeared, the price of gold was hovering between $280 and $300 per ounce, lower than at anytime during the previous twenty years. Forbes Magazine was right. For centuries one ounce of gold could buy a fine men's suit complete with vest.

In 1998, however, with the price of gold down to $280, it would take four ounces of gold to buy the same fine suit (see writer's note that follows). In the late 1990s, by the suit standard the price of gold was 25 % of what it should have been

On July 1, 2006, with the price of gold at $610, by the suit standard, gold was still cheap, though not as cheap as it was in 1998. Now it would only take two ounces of gold to buy a fine man's suit, instead of four. Still, while a discount of 50 % is not as preferable as 75 %, gold nonetheless still remained in the bargain category.

Writer's note #1: *It must be remembered we are talking about a fine man's suit, of an excellent quality English gabardine with a vest. Those who shop at department stores never see such suits except rarely and then only on others. And it is those who wear such suits who also possess the gold we read and hear about.*

Writer's note #2: *Since we are on the subject, a <u>really fine</u> man's suit from a Savile Row bespoke tailor will now cost between 5 and 6 ounces of gold (~$3,600 to $4,300). This figure may in fact actually portend what the price of gold will be when gold runs free.*

Vulture advice: Buy your gold now and you may have a shot at such a suit later. For information on such tailoring, Thomas Mahon's **www.englishcut.com** is a wonderful and informative introduction to this special world.

There is a reason for Forbes' observation in 1998 that for the first time in centuries, the centuries-old relationship between the price of gold and a fine man's suit had broken down (for those so inclined, this might be a possible personal arbitrage opportunity still with some legs).

In the 1990s, collusion between Central Banks and investment banks had finally forced down the "free-market" price of gold. In so doing, investment banks had convinced the Central Banks that they had a better use for Central Bank gold. And they did. At least it was better for the investment banks. It was also to be the last time the Central Bankers were to see their gold.

WHEN CENTRAL BANKS
AND INVESTMENT BANKS
COLLUDE IN MANAGING GOLD
ONE IS GETTING PAID
ONE IS GETTING LAID

At the time the Forbes article was published, the annual demand for gold was 4000 tonnes (metric tons) per year. Since gold mining produces around 2500 tonnes yearly, there is an annual shortfall in production of 1500 tonnes, 60 % of production.

If grain harvests were continually short of demand by 60 %, grain prices would be skyrocketing and those holding grain would be trying to take advantage of this shortfall to make windfall profits; loaves of bread would be getting smaller and smaller and their cost increasingly dear. But this was not grain, it was gold.

The speculative frenzy surrounding gold should have been spectacular. But it wasn't. There were no spectacular profits in the making on gold's explosive upswing because there was no upswing. In fact, the very opposite happened. Hundreds of tonnes of gold were soon to appear on the market, unexpectedly depressing the price of gold even further.

THE CENTRAL BANKS WERE ON THE MOVE

On May 8, 1999 Chancellor Gordon Brown of Britain suddenly announced that Britain would be selling 415 tonnes of gold, fully 58 % of its total reserves, leaving Britain with only 300 tonnes, the lowest amount of any major country in the world. Eleven days earlier, on April 27, 1999, Brown had requested the IMF sell $10 billion of its gold on the open market.

What would cause Britain to sell off 58 % of its gold reserves, gold that had taken centuries and such pains to accumulate by way of positive balances of trade and ill-gotten gains forced from its empire of imperialism? What would cause its Central Banker to ask other institutions to do the same, sell significant portions of their gold when the price of gold was at all time lows?

Perhaps the British Central Bankers had decided it was high time to replenish their wardrobes with bespoke tailored suits from Savile Row and to drive gold even lower so as to arbitrage their wardrobe purchases in time for the new millennium to be celebrated at the revitalized Canary Wharf complex. Perhaps, but the theory rings hollow and there is another theory afoot.

The radical action taken by the Bank of England was not to raise money. The purpose of the gold sales by the Central Bank of England was to drive the price of gold lower still in order to avert a financial meltdown. The price of gold had to be lowered quickly and the announcement of gold auction by the Bank of England of over half its gold reserves was required in order to do so.

The rumor in London at the time was that New York investment bank Goldman Sachs had a 1,000 tonne short gold position in the market and if the price of gold were to rise they would suffer catastrophic losses.

Bank of England Governor Eddie George later spoke to Nicholas J. Morrell, CEO of Lonmin Plc, about the sale of Britain's gold and said:

> *We looked into the abyss if the gold price rose further. A further rise would have taken down one or several trading houses, which might have taken down all the rest in their wake. Therefore at any price, at any cost, the Central Banks had to quell the gold price, manage it. It was very difficult to get the gold price under control but we have now succeeded. The US Fed was very active in getting the gold price down. So was the U.K.*

The rumors also included speculation that Goldman Sachs had shorted the gold on behalf of the US government; that the US government was actively colluding with Goldman Sachs to manipulate the price of gold, and the market had turned against them.

One month after Britain had announced it would sell the majority of its gold (and in such a way as to depress the price in the process), the following comments were made in the House of Commons on June 16, 1999 by Sir Peter Tapsall.

Sir Peter Tapsall's words bear repeating:

> *I regard the decision to sell 415 of the 715 tonnes of our gold reserves as a reckless act, which goes against Britain's national interest. The sale of that crucial element of the United Kingdom's reserve assets will weaken our scope to operate independently, reduce our influence in international financial institutions and diminish the United Kingdom as a world financial power.*
>
> *The immediate effect has been the loss of £400 million of our taxpayers' reserves, and so far the only beneficiaries of this event have been the foreign finance houses, which have been shorting the gold market...[rumors] that some of those famous foreign finance houses have shorted gold to a huge amount—vastly greater than the tonnage of sales contemplated by the Bank of England—and that it was therefore vital*

for them for the gold price to fall substantially so that they could close their positions and take huge profits.

A financial crisis had brought the world to the brink of disaster. Once again, the gamblers and speculators in charge of today's investment banks had leveraged their positions in such a way as to endanger the financial health of nations and indeed the world.

Once again, government had come to the rescue of the private sector, the investment bankers. The lesson was again clearly evident—the even hand of the marketplace is reserved only for the lesser players; those who sit at the head of the table get a pass, gratis of course, paid for by a citizenry that doesn't enjoy the luxury of such privileges.

The collapse of the present financial edifice can come from many directions and from many causes. So will it be in the time of the vulture. When the abyss is no longer avoidable, it may be a dollar crisis that pushes us over the edge or it might be a failure of a major investment bank such as Goldman Sachs, JP Morgan, Citicorp, or Deutsche Bank or another overleveraged hedge fund like Long Term Capital Management or the inability of a small bank somewhere in the daisy chain of financial institutions to meet its obligations on a Monday morning.

In 1931 the failure of an Austrian bank, Credit Anstalt, set in motion a series of bank failures that was to plunge the world into the abyss now known as the Great Depression. Who knows what will be the cause this time? What bank? What currency? What default? What event?

Only one thing is sure. The present financial edifice, built on an inherently unstable foundation of paper money and ever-increasing mountains of debt, is vulnerable as never before. It may be a sudden movement or a gust of wind or a sonic boom; but whatever it is:

IT CAN NO LONGER BE SAID IT WILL BE UNEXPECTED

2012 UPDATE: On July 17, 2012, an article in The Telegraph UK confirmed the rumors as to what happened to England's gold in 1999:

Britain's gold reserves were sold at a ludicrously low price...the sale of the majority of Britain's gold reserves for prices between $256 and $296 an ounce, only to watch it soar so far as $1,615 per ounce today...It seemed almost as if the Treasury was trying to achieve the lowest price possible for the public's gold. It was.

One of the most popular trading plays of the late 1990s was the carry trade, particularly the gold carry trade... In this a bank would borrow gold from another financial institution for a set period, and pay a token sum relative to the overall value of that gold for the privilege.

Once control of the gold had been passed over, the bank would then immediately sell it for its full market value. The proceeds would be invested in an alternative product which was predicted to generate a better return over the period than gold which was enduring a spell of relative price stability, even decline.

At the end of the allotted period, the bank would sell its investment and use the proceeds to buy back the amount of gold it had originally borrowed. This gold would be returned to the lender. The borrowing bank would trouser the difference between the two prices.

This plan worked brilliantly when gold fell and the other asset – for the bank at the heart of this case, yen-backed securities – rose. When the prices moved the other way, the banks were in trouble.

This is what had happened on an enormous scale by early 1999. One globally significant US bank in particular is understood to have been heavily short on two tonnes of gold, enough to call into question its solvency if redemption occurred at the prevailing price.

...Faced with the prospect of a global collapse in the banking system, the Chancellor took the decision to bail out the banks by dumping Britain's gold, forcing the price down and allowing the banks to buy back gold at a profit, thus meeting their borrowing obligations.

The rumors of which I wrote in 2006/2007 have now been confirmed. In 1999, England had sold over 50% of its gold to bail out the banks. For 300 years, bankers and governments have been co-conspirators in a highly successful ponzi-scheme to indebt society and to profit thereby. That scheme is collapsing. Be thankful.

Section III

SECTION IV

BEFORE THE YEN CARRY TRADE THERE WAS THE GOLD CARRY TRADE AFTER THE GOLD CARRY TRADE THERE MIGHT BE NOT MUCH TRADE AT ALL

Topic 18

Grandpa, is the price of gold really rigged?
Yes, Virginia it is.
But how do they do it?
Well, that's a long story
Tell me, Grandpa, I really want to know.
OK, Virginia, this is how it happened

Shortly after the US de-linked the dollar from gold, the US decided to force the price of gold lower. The now fiat-dollar looked good when the price of gold did not; and when gold was high, the paper dollar looked less trustworthy. And nothing, absolutely nothing is as important as trust when a confidence game is being run.

In the 1970s, initial attempts to cap the gold price failed because US inflation rates spiraled upwards just as the US and the IMF were selling millions of ounces of gold in the attempt to force gold down. Investors instead flocked to gold to protect them from inflation as gold prices exploded upwards.

In the 1980s, then chairman of the Fed Paul Volker raised interest rates to 21.5 % which slowed the US economy down enough so inflation rates returned to normal. This was when another plan to cap the price of gold was put into effect.

This plan would work. Eventually, it would work so well that it would distort the 1:1 relationship between an ounce of gold and a man's fine suit of clothes. As Forbes Magazine noted in 1998, gold was so cheap it would now take four ounces of gold to buy such a suit. Instead of a 1:1 relationship, it was now 1:4. For four hundred years this relationship stood the test of time. Now, it did not.

In the late 1990s, by the suit standard, the price of gold was 75 % lower than it should have been. The US government in collusion with Central Banks and investment banks had finally succeeded in forcing down the price of gold fourfold.

This Is How It Was Done: Beginning in the 1980s, the US Fed and other Central Banks started to loan their gold reserves to investment banks at the very low interest rate of 1 %. The investment banks would sell the gold, investing the proceeds in interest-bearing bonds paying higher, for example, 6 % interest. The 5 % spread between interest rates was their profit.

This continual new supply of gold on the market forced gold prices lower over time, which is what both the Central Banks and investment banks wanted. The Central Banks wanted gold lower because it made inflation less visible and their paper currencies appear more stable. The investment banks wanted gold lower because when it came time to repay their gold loans they could buy gold at a lower price and make even more money.

This became known as the gold-carry trade, a forerunner of the Japanese yen-carry trade that was to come later. In both instances the original asset (gold or yen) would be borrowed at low interest (1 % for gold, 0 % for yen) and would be sold, with the proceeds reinvested in assets that offered higher rates of return.

The only risk was that if the underlying asset (gold or yen) rose in price before the time came due to repay the loan, the underlying asset would have to be repurchased at a higher price, incurring perhaps serious losses for the borrower. This risk was later to become more than just apparent.

As long as prices stayed low, the gold carry-trade was a win for the Central Banks wanting to suppress the price of gold and the investment banks that were handsomely profiting once more at the trough of government largesse.

The extent of these gold loans was hidden, as the Central Banks did not want known the level of their collusion in the illegal manipulation of gold markets; and if it weren't for the efforts of Frank AJ Veneroso, the real volume of gold loans would never have been discovered.

Frank Veneroso is the author of the Gold Book Annual, probably the most comprehensive study and analysis of gold markets available today. One of the world's foremost financial analysts, Veneroso's clients have included the World Bank, the Organization of American States, sovereign nations and global money managers.

Frank Veneroso is also chief investment strategist for RCM Global Investors, the equity investment arm of Allianz Dresdner, the giant German insurance conglomerate which also owns the PIMCO bond funds, the bailiwick of Bill Gross.

It was in compiling the statistics on gold markets that Veneroso discovered that the Central Banks were hiding the vast majority of their gold loans from public view. Veneroso estimated that by the late 1990s, the highly lucrative and still hidden gold-carry trade amounted to 10,000 to 15,000 tonnes of gold.

The Central Banks pointed to their books which showed receipts showing large amounts of gold on deposit. What Veneroso suspected and found to be true, however, was that the gold wasn't there. Ten to fifteen thousand tonnes of gold, an amount far larger than the Central Banks would admit, had been loaned to the investment banks in order to suppress the price of gold and now, in Veneroso's opinion, were never coming back.

CENTRAL BANK GOLD
NOW GONE WITH THE WIND

Veneroso noted that the amount of physical gold lent, 10,000-15,000 tonnes, is far too large for investment banks to repurchase without causing the price of gold to explosively rise, the very result the Central Banks had set out to prevent.

The success of the gold-carry trade had led to its failure. Now, at the cost of almost half of their gold reserves, the Central Banks are left only with promissory notes from investment banks instead of the tons of physical gold they had once possessed.

Whereas someone you know, perhaps even yourself, may in the very near future be forced out of their foreclosed home by bank order, rest assured that the investment banks will suffer no consequence for not repaying the gold they borrowed from Central Banks, gold that belonged to the nations that lent it, not its Central Bankers. In matters of finance, especially, the "even hand of justice" is reserved primarily for those that cannot afford it.

It is estimated that in the past, Central Banks' holdings of gold totaled 32,000 tonnes; and Veneroso's figures show that perhaps 50 % of that is gone. This newly-discovered charade of Central Bank bookkeeping is as fraudulent as Enron's; and as with Enron, the bookkeepers were complicit in the deception.

Instead of Arthur Anderson, the now defunct and disgraced accounting firm that certified Enron's books, this time the complicit agency was the International Monetary Fund. In April 2006, the IMF finally admitted that its accounting rules allow member nations to double count their gold reserves. That gold lent out is allowed under IMF regulations to be "legally" counted as still being on deposit.

This is like a bank loaning a customer $100 million dollars and being allowed to still count that $100 million as being on deposit. This is fraud at the highest level but because it is at the highest level, no one will ever be held accountable. Those at the highest levels make the laws. They do not abide by them.

However, the fact that many Central Banks no longer have significant gold reserves is of critical importance—for it means that Central Banks are running out of physical gold to sell in order to suppress gold's price. In any war, when supplies wane, so too do the odds of success.

By the end of August 1942, Montgomery was ready himself. He knew that Rommel was very short of fuel and that the Germans could not sustain a long campaign.

- The Battle of El Alamein

Veneroso has estimated that Central Banks have only three years' supply of gold left to contain gold's price. Veneroso also believes Central Banks will capitulate before that time.

It is therefore likely that within one to two years, the US and other Central Banks will cease their attempts to fix the price of gold and choose to keep what little gold they may have left.

When that happens, the price of gold will explode upwards and it will then be discovered that many Central Banks had already switched sides in an epic battle that is now still in progress.

2012 UPDATE: The central bank shift from net sellers to net buyers of gold in 2011 is an indication debt-based paper economies are beginning to unravel. In the 12 months ending March 31, 2012, central banks bought 250% more gold than the year before. This trend will bankrupt the bankers before it's over.

PHYSICAL GOLD
THE DEMAND THAT CANNOT BE FILLED

Topic 19

Buy gold now while the central bankers are still selling it at a discount because when they stop, the price of gold will skyrocket upwards as never before.

Financial markets are, by and large, like the paper currencies on which they are based, artificial inventions designed primarily to facilitate speculation. The amount of paper money bet daily on the price of gold far exceeds the actual physical amount of gold available.

On the New York Mercantile Exchange division, COMEX, the trade in gold is settled mainly in paper money, not physical gold. This is also true of the Japanese futures market, the Tokyo Commodities Exchange, TOCOM.

It is not necessarily true, however, of the London Bullion Market Association, LBMA, where physical gold changes hands far more often. And because of that, the London market is a far better gauge of gold's real movements, not the paper trails left elsewhere by speculators and those wishing to distort what the real market might show.

In an article published in the UK newspaper, The Telegraph, June 5, 2006, it was reported that **the Union Bank of Switzerland revealed gold bullion purchases are eight times higher than believed**.

The article also stated the "extra volume in gold buying has been channeled through the London Bullion Market Association, eclipsing the COMEX futures market in New York, usually monitored by speculators for clues".

If anybody knows the extent of the world's real gold trade, it is UBS. The Union Bank of Switzerland, the world's biggest gold trader, manages over $1 trillion in wealth for its private clients. UBS estimated that funds and investors were allocating 20 % of their commodity portfolios to precious metals.

This is a much higher percentage than reported by Goldman Sachs. The Goldman Sachs Commodity Index shows a gold and silver weighting of 2.27 % as compared to a 74 % weighting in the energy sector.

It must be remembered however that Goldman Sachs is believed by many to be complicit in fixing the price of gold along with the US Government; and a lower rate of precious metals allocation would tend to lower investor interest in this sector.

In the June 5, 2006 article, UBS also warned that while the long term outlook for gold was decidedly positive, there was an intermediate risk of a global economic downturn that would drag "gold down in an avalanche sale of all commodities"; an avalanche that gold would ultimately survive before embarking again on a strong upward path.

The previous mid-May 2006 market loss of $2 trillion was not the avalanche spoken of by Union Bank. May's correction was only a pre-avalanche trial run of what might be. The economic global downturn when an "avalanche sale of all commodities" might occur is what we believe will be in the third and final stage of economic-collapse.

The collapse of stocks and commodities in 2008 may well be the *global economic downturn that would drag "gold down in an avalanche sale of all commodities"; an avalanche that gold would ultimately survive before embarking again on a strong upward path.*

Indeed, in 2008 gold fell from its previous high of $1,033 to $740 before fighting its way back up again to $1,000 in February 2009. But when this happened, gold was again forced below $900 as European central banks sold 220 tons of gold in order to keep gold from rising further.

The bankers with their empire of monopoly paper money now at risk, are selling the gold reserves of European nations in a last ditch attempt to preserve their immense wealth and power. Their attempts to do so, however, are futile as every ton they sell is one ton closer to the day when they will have no gold left to sell.

When allied troops stormed the beaches at Normandy, it was the beginning of the end for Nazi Germany. But between Normandy and Berlin was a great distance in miles, blood, and time. So it is with the battle between paper money and gold.

Paper money had its day as did Nazi Germany. During the expansion of the 1980s and the boom times of the 1990s, it appeared that paper's triumph was complete, and gold an outdated relic.

Indeed, from 1981-2000 and especially so between 1996 and 2000, paper was the unquestioned victor. In the late 1990s, the price of gold was but ¼ of what it should have been. Only its most ardent believers and supporters had faith that gold's day would come.

GOLD'S DAY IS ALMOST HERE

2012 UPDATE: In 2008 when the global economy collapsed, bankers intervened and forced the price of gold from $1,000 per ounce down to $740; and, today, bankers have again forced the price of gold below what markets would dictate.

In September 2011, as the European debt crisis worsened, gold reflected the systemic distress by rising 27% in only two months. This rapid rise forced bankers to slash gold lease rates into negative territory in order to bring gold back into the $1500/$1600 range.

But just as gold would resume its rise in 2009, gold will again move far, far higher. This is a battle of paradigms. Gold has risen from $250 per ounce in 2001 to $1600 today because of increasing economic uncertainty. That uncertainty is rising and so will the price of gold.

THE BULL BREAKS LOOSE
GOLD MAKES A MOVE
AND FALLS WITH THE CROWD

Topic 20

Just because someone's at the steering wheel doesn't mean we're under control. We're speeding downhill and the high rate of our descent makes any attempt at control a possibility the very opposite could happen.

After falling in price for twenty years, gold's ascent began in the new millennium in the $280s and by January 2006 gold had pushed past $530, an increase of 89 % over a six year period. However in the spring of 2006, by early May, gold moved quickly upwards, accelerating from $530 to $730, a 38 % increase in only four months.

The rapid rise of gold ignited both the hopes of those believing in gold and the fears of those suppressing its price. For twenty years, the paper money cartel had successfully forced the price of gold lower via the gold-carry trade. Since 2000, however, their efforts had been less successful though they still persisted in opposing gold's progress.

But in 2006, gold's stubborn ascent had pushed through all resistance on its way to its top in early May at $730. But from mid-May to mid-June, gold fell back to where it had begun the year in the $530s.

What occurred, however, as gold plummeted downward is as important in the war between paper money and gold as the Battle of Stalingrad or the Battle at El Alamein between Nazi Germany and the allies—when critical battles were fought that were ultimately to determine the outcome of the war itself.

In their struggle to force down gold, the supporters of paper money, the coalition of the deceiving, the Central Banks of the US, the UK, Japan, and others need to pick their battles very carefully; for although they represent enormous collective power, they are up against a far superior opponent—the marketplace.

Because of this, the New York Mercantile Exchange division, COMEX, is the coalition's choice of battlefields. At the COMEX, trades are settled primarily by money, not delivery of physicals.

The strength of the coalition of the deceiving is an endless supply of paper money, their weakness - their limited supplies of physical gold. COMEX therefore gives the coalition a slight edge in an uphill war.

What follows is an extraordinary tale of what occurred during one week, between June 6th and June 13th at COMEX as gold fell from its mid-May 2006 top. The account was posted on the internet on June 19 by Dan Norcini, a gold futures trader at COMEX.

Like the Zapruder film of the Kennedy assassination, what Dan Norcini witnessed in the gold futures pit at COMEX provides details that we would otherwise never have known, details that give clues to shifts that happen only in the heat of battle, clues that indicate who the eventual victor will be.

As evident from Dan Norcini's account, the COMEX gold futures market is like no other market. In other markets, commercial sellers seek a higher price for their wares. In the gold futures market at COMEX, most sellers of gold are not seeking higher prices; **instead they are seeking to force the price of gold lower**.

But during this critical time period, Dan Norcini witnessed a turning point in the war between paper and gold, a war that will end in paper's capitulation and gold's triumph. This is Norcini's amazing account:

REMARKABLE DEVELOPMENT IN THE GOLD MARKET

By: Dan Norcini

- Posted Monday, 19 June 2006
- http://news.goldseek.com/DanNorcini/1150729200.php

Over the past years that I have been privileged to participate in this fledgling generational bull market in gold, I have written a goodly number of essays detailing the Commitments of Traders [COT] reports and analyzing how that relates to the price action experienced in the gold futures pit at the Comex.

Having been at this game for a long time now, I can usually get a pretty good feel for who is doing what during the course of the week by comparing the price action in the pit against the previous week's COT [Commitments of Traders] report and looking at the long term trend of a market.

In what I consider to be "normal" markets, a rising market in an established bull trend will usually see the bulk of the speculators, both large and small, on the long [up] side with the bulk of the commercials taking the opposite or short [down] side.

That only makes sense as commercials/producers are using the speculator buying to implement scale-up selling programs to lock in profits. They sell a little here and a little there and continue to do so as prices rise, assuring themselves of a profit and minimizing risk which the speculators are more than willing to assume in exchange for an opportunity to make a profit. The higher the market rises, the happier these true or bona-fide hedgers are as that means higher selling prices for their goods.

Over the past years in this gold market we have witnessed some anomalous patterns in the open interest activity that I have detailed in great extent in various essays I have published out on the web.

Unlike "normal" markets, the pattern for gold has been for the commercials to meet determined speculator buying in gold with fierce resistance all the way up in a manner that is normally not consistent with price maximizing selling.

Upward progress is met, not with commercials standing aside and allowing the funds to drive the market north and then selling lightly into that buying only enough to cover their immediate hedging needs, but rather with fierce and determined selling that fights and contends against all upward progress. I have therefore come to expect this pattern as the norm in the gold market.

Imagine my surprise then to learn from today's release of the COT [Commitments of Traders] report that the commercial category went even one step further than I had come to expect from them. Their normal pattern has been to sell with steady determination but only into rising prices as they attempt to cap the price rise and resist the upward progress of the metal.

Once the fund buying has abated or stalled, they then launch a counterattack of heavy offers which overpower the bidders in the market. This has the intended effect of causing a quick retreat by the locals who front run their offers and proceed to knock the market down into the sell-stops below which are then automatically touched off turning speculators into sellers.

The process then feeds on itself producing an avalanche of selling which trips all the short term technical oscillators and has the black boxes lighting up the computerized platforms with even more speculator sell orders which soon turns into a veritable blood letting.

The cartel of commercials then use this forced speculator selling to buy back or cover the short positions they had built up over the course of the price rise congratulating themselves for having fleeced the momentum based trading funds who chased the market higher. We have seen this pattern repeat itself going all the way back to 2001.

What is quite extraordinary about today's report was that it detailed something which I have not seen during the course of this entire bull market since 2001, namely, increasing short sales by the commercial category in the midst of a falling market – not just a falling market, but a precipitously falling market at that. This is a startling new development.

What is even more remarkable is that the big trading funds, instead of dumping their longs into the lap of the waiting commercial cartel, actually appear to have been buying on the way down! This also is a FIRST! In other words, we have seen in one week a COMPLETE REVERSAL of the norm of the last 5 years in the gold market.

As a matter of fact what I had been expecting to see was a REDUCTION in the net short position of the commercial category and a reduction in the net long position of the trading funds. I assumed that the gold cartel would dupe the trading funds into establishing a huge number of new short positions even as that same category sharply cut the number of long positions. I also assumed that the same thing would happen among the small spec category.

What actually happened was the exact opposite except for the small specs who ditched more shorts than they did longs! The big trading funds INCREASED their net long position as the market fell – something they have not done throughout the history of this past bull market.

Instead of piling on a ton of new shorts, the trading funds added only a bit more than 700 new shorts and almost 4,000 new longs into the price weakness. Could it be that this category is finally wising up and actually learning to beat the cartel at its own game? We will have to see but the fact that this has occurred at all is nothing short of astonishing.

Notice the data from last week's COT [Commitments of Traders] report and this current's week COT report.

Let me try to put it another way. The COT [Commitments of Traders] report covers the activity of the traders from the Tuesday of the week past to the Tuesday of the current week. In other words, if we want to learn who was doing what from Tuesday to Tuesday we can get a very good picture from looking at that report.

Let me try to put it another way. The COT [Commitments of Traders] report covers the activity of the traders from the Tuesday of the week past to the Tuesday of the current week. In other words, if we want to learn who was doing what from Tuesday to Tuesday we can get a very good picture from looking at that report.

COMMERCIALS		NET POSITION	SMALL SPECS		NET POSITION
LONGS	SHORTS		LONGS	SHORTS	
51,439	180,808	-129,369	48,122	14,649	+33,473
51,699	186,100	-134,401	46,632	11,518	+35,114

DATE	TOTAL OPEN INTEREST	FUNDS		NET POSITION	SPREADERS
		LONGS	SHORTS		
6/6/2006	283,161	134,649	38,753	+95,896	
6/13/2006	288,981	138,766	39,479	+99,287	

Unfortunately the report does not tell us who was doing what on Wednesday, Thursday and Friday of the current week. That will show up in the following week. Still, we can get enough information to correctly identify the transition of players for a week's interval of time.

Having established this we can now go back to the gold chart and look at the price action of the market from Tuesday of last week, 6-6-2006 to the Tuesday of the current week, 6-13-2006.

On Monday of last week, the price of August Comex Gold closed the session at 648.70. This will be our starting point for the analysis that follows since the COT [Commitments of Traders] report will show us who did what from the following day until Tuesday of this week as compared against the price action of gold.

The next day, Tuesday, 6-6-2006, gold dropped down to 634.70. Wednesday it went down to 632.60. Thursday it took another huge hit and closed down at 613.80. Friday it closed down at 612.80. The following Monday, at the start of this week, it continued its  downward progress and closed at 611.30. Tuesday, the final day of this week which is covered by the COT report, it was walloped for a gargantuan hit of $55 closing all the way down at 566.80.

It was further mauled overnight beginning in the afternoon Access session on into Tuesday evening when it began to gets it footing in the late afternoon Asian action and early morning European trading session. To sum up – gold went straight down from Tuesday of last week thru Tuesday of this week to a tune of a loss of $81.90, and if you include the Tuesday overnight action, a whopping loss of $102.30 in one week!

To further amplify on what I have described previously - Whereas the normal pattern of the last five years in gold as I have described above would have expected us to see the commercial cartel covering or reducing their shorts and booking profits, the exact opposite occurred – the commercial shorts, aka known as the gold cartel, SOLD THE ENTIRE WAY DOWN – instead of REDUCING the number of their shorts and booking profits they actually PUT ON MORE OF THEM!

The COT [Commitments of Traders] report reveals that they added a total of 5,282 BRAND NEW SHORTS as the price of gold collapsed. They have NEVER done this before during any time in this bull market in gold since it began way back in 2001.

What does this mean? – quite simple – it means that there was a concerted effort on the part of this group of short sellers to FORCE THE GOLD PRICE DOWN. They had absolutely no interest in booking profits on existing shorts as the price tumbled some $100.

This is a stunning development as it clearly indicates a concerted attempt to derail what was becoming a runaway bull market in the gold price that was threatening to garner far too much public attention. Remember - gold's perennial function is to serve as the financial "canary in the coal mine" which alerts the workers to hidden, toxic dangers.

Quite simply, gold's stunning rally to $730 in the matter of a few months time was sending shock waves through the corridors of the monetary elites who were "looking into the abyss" if gold continued its meteoric rise. Something had to be done and quickly or this thing was going to get out of hand.

Along that line, this past week I sent some comments up to my good friend Bill Murphy over at GATA's [Gold Anti-Trust Action Committee] fine site, **www.lemetropolecafe.com** detailing both in written and in visual chart form what appeared to me to be a deliberate assault that was being launched against the gold market beginning in the thin and illiquid conditions of the aftermarket access trading session as soon as it opened for the resumption of trading in the afternoons. Bill included those in his daily Midas reports. Also, my trading buddy and good pal Jim Sinclair (**www.jsmineset.com**) had posted the same comments along with the price charts detailing the attack as shown on the 30 minute interval chart.

As a trader who trades exclusively in the CBOT's [Chicago Board of Trade] full-sized electronic gold contract every single day, I am quite attuned to the normal order flow into that "pit". What caught my eye immediately beginning last week and continuing with the assault on gold early this week, was the huge size of sell offers that came flooding into those pits late last week and earlier this week during the normally comparatively quiet afternoon session.

Offers of 500+ to sell were relentlessly pounding the CBOT [Chicago Board of Trade] electronic gold contract. One enormous sell order of 943 hit the pit much to my stunned amazement. I found myself talking out loud to myself saying, "What in the world is going on here? Did I miss something happening in the world? Did someone Central Banker or Fed governor say something? Who in the heck is selling like this?"

To give you some perspective – I rarely see buy or sell orders in the early afternoon session exceeding 100 contracts going either way. Clearly some entity was attempting to mercilessly pound the price down into lower levels looking to run stops in the thin conditions and set off a cascade of further selling which would then be expected to carry over into the TOCOM [Tokyo Commodities Exchange] session that evening driving the price even lower as Japanese selling took over.

So the question becomes, who would do such a thing and why?

Then it all began to make perfect sense if one understands what both Jim Sinclair and Bill Murphy and the GATA [Gold Anti-Trust Action Committee] gang had been saying about this recent price decline in gold, namely, that it was an orchestrated and deliberate attack by the Central Bankers of the West to break the back of the gold market and defuse the warning message that gold was sounding abroad.

In our opinion, it started with the Bank of England either mobilizing its own gold supplies or gold from the IMF. This gold was then used to temporarily flood the market with extra supply with which to overwhelm the soaring investment demand thereby knocking the price of gold, and other commodities sharply downward to give the intended effect that fears of inflation due to commodity price rises had been effectively contained.

In order to effect the most carnage on gold, this surreptitiously mobilized supply of extra gold had to be accompanied by a concerted and well-coordinated effort on the part of the Western Central Bankers and some of their allies of tough anti-inflation talk giving the impression that the CB's [Central Banks] were going to be especially vigilant to nip any inflation genie in the bud.

Think about this a bit and see if we can put two and two together. If you knew in advance that the BOE [Bank of England] was about to make a move to derail the surging copper market and bail out its friends at the LME [London Metals Exchange] which was on the verge of witnessing a default among some of its members who had stupidly sold short into a roaring bull market in copper, and you knew that they would also do this by launching an all out assault on the base metals and especially on the gold price using mobilized Central Bank vault gold, what do you think you could conclude?

Answer – the price of gold was going to fall sharply as it would be temporarily overwhelmed by the extra supply hitting the market. If you knew this would you not sell with complete reckless abandon? Would you not attempt to chase the market down as far as you could pushing into one set of sell stops after another?

Would you not do this in the hopes of wreaking as much carnage on the market as possible and then eventually clean up by buying all those shorts back after you had broken the back of nearly every would-be gold bull on the planet? I know I sure would have! You would be a complete nitwit not to recognize such a gift horse being dropped into your lap!

Well, that is exactly what I believe occurred. The BOE [Bank of England] in conjunction with their cohorts at the Fed, would have tipped off its agents, or better yet, would have plotted with its agents Goldman Sachs, et al, that it was about to mobilize its gold or the IMF's gold and dump it onto the market.

In the meantime Goldman Sachs and friends were unleashed to smash the paper markets in gold at both the Comex and the CBOT [Chicago Board of Trade], and run as many speculators out of it as possible while seeking to inflict the most technical damage possible on the price charts.

The intended effect was to be to so completely dishearten and discourage the public and the investment funds from buying gold that it would suffer an ignominious death and fall off the radar screens of investors. That would effectively get it out of the headlines and remove the pesky metal's telltale warning signs about the true state of the global economy. No more gold stories equals happy Central Bankers.

There is no doubt that the plan worked to near perfection – I have never seen so much near total despair and disillusionment among the friends of gold as I witnessed this past Tuesday and early Wednesday. Out of everywhere, as if on cue, analysts confidently pronounced that the bull market in gold and in commodities was over, finis, kaput!

However, a funny thing happened on the way to the forum. Someone showed up to meet the brazen sellers and began to buy in huge lots. Gold quickly ricocheted off the $545-$550 level running all the way back to near $590 in two days.

Today, Friday, 6-16-2006, when the same group of sellers once again attempted to break the back of the gold market which had come roaring back in overnight trade in both Asia and in Europe, and began their coordinated selling assault during the New York trading session (what else is new), out of nowhere buying came out of everywhere forcing them to beat a hasty retreat.

Gold, which at one point had been knocked down $20 off its overnight highs, came back with a vengeance stuffing the shorts and forcing them back out as it closed the session in remarkable fashion for a Friday afternoon.

The strong close augurs well for next week although gold did suffer some pretty heavy technical damage this week as a result of the attack. It will take our friend some time to repair the damage suffered but it demonstrated true grit this week by coming back from such a fierce beating in so noble a fashion to end the week.

One has to understand that as a result of the work of GATA [Gold Anti-Trust Action Committee] and especially the conference in the Klondike that the big physical market buyers know full well what is going on in the gold market and were laying in wait for Goldman and company. And why should they not?

If one understands the war involving gold and knows that there exists a group of entities who are intent on smashing the price of gold and will utilize all the resources at their disposal, why not wait for them to pull one of their stunts, step aside for a while, let them knock the price back down and then buy all that you can fit into your boats at a greatly reduced price level.

After all, if you are determined to own gold and increase your holdings of it as the Russians, Chinese and Arab interests are, why not let the fools make it available to you at a nice big discount and then load the boat compliments of your short-sighted but "generous" benefactors?

In conclusion, we will need to see the price action this next week and the COT [Commitments of Traders] report next Friday along with the daily open interest reports to see if the gold cartel is forced to cover those brand new shorts, many of which are underwater at this point and whether the funds will now trade this gold market a bit more intelligently.

We want to see if gold can hold the recent lows on any possible subsequent revisiting of those lows. If so, and if especially the volume dries up in comparison to that of the day when the lows were made, then the bottom is definitely in and gold will start its next leg up from this region after a period of base building.

We know that down at those levels there are huge buyers waiting in the physical market who want to obtain gold at what they consider to be a "value" area. That is the key. Those guys want all the cheap gold they can get and will pounce on it at a price they are happy with.

If the CB's [Central Banks] want to dump more gold on the market, those big buyers will be more than happy to relieve them of it all. Heaven help the new shorts in this market if that gang of physical market buyers decides this is as cheap as gold is going to get again.

June 16, 2006

Dan Norcini

The thirty-year war between paper money and gold is drawing near its end. The US Federal Reserve and assorted Central Banks were very successful between 1981 and 2000 in forcing the price of gold down, albeit at the cost of losing much of their gold.

Since then it has been a different story. The bull market in commodities lifted gold along with its base metal cousins and as global uncertainties became more pronounced, the precious metal developed a momentum of its own and exploded upwards in the spring of 2006.

And, as Dan Norcini's story shows, gold forces are now gathering strength and growing more confident. The day is not far off when the growing confidence in gold will overpower the waning belief in paper assets.

As Dan Norcini reported, there are now significant buyers waiting in the wings to buy gold at a "value level", buyers from the Middle East, Russia, and China. And who are these buyers?

They are no less than the Central Banks of Russia, China, and the Middle East now seeking to diversify out of the US dollar into gold.

THE TIME OF THE VULTURE IS AT HAND

> **2012 UPDATE:** Dan Norcini's epic account about 'the battle in the pits', e.g. COMEX, over gold is as relevant today as it was then. If anything, the battle has become even more intense as the bankers' end grows nearer. What Norcini portrayed then is a glimpse into a protracted struggle which is not yet over. It will be, however. 'When' is the only question. The outcome is certain.

CENTRAL BANKS
CAUGHT IN THE CROSSHAIRS
ONCE JOINED TOGETHER
NOW NO LONGER

Topic 21

The shift from a male hierarchical paradigm to one equally balanced between male and female is reflected in the ascendance of the East and the relative decline of the West. The shift will be no less significant and no less difficult between nations than it is between men and women.

The alliance formed thirty years ago between Central Banks is no more. What gave rise to that alliance no longer exists. In times of change, agendas change and alliances shift; and in 2006 the agendas of Central Banks changed significantly.

When the US officially de-linked the US dollar from gold in 1973, it affected the value of all currencies. Under Bretton-Woods, currencies were linked to the US dollar and the US dollar was convertible to gold; therefore prior to 1973 all currencies were indirectly connected to gold. After 1973, this was no longer so.

If another country had misspent its gold reserves as had the US, it would have suffered significant sanctions imposed by the IMF. But because it was the US that was the miscreant, economically and militarily the most powerful nation in the world, there were no such repercussions.

Indeed, the very opposite occurred. All Central Banks including the IMF were forced to ally with the US in defending paper money in the new US-induced era of global fiat-currency.

The overriding concern of Central Banks in the aftermath of the de-linking of currencies from gold was the stability of their currencies. Forced against their will into an era of "floating" currencies, Central Banks of necessity focused on maintaining the stability of their newly fiat moneys.

DEFLATIONISTS BELIEVE THAT
WHAT GOES UP MUST COME DOWN
CENTRAL BANKERS ARE PAID TO DENY IT

It is important to remember that only the US misspent its gold reserves, that no other nation had done so; but because the US dollar was the mechanism by which all currencies were anchored to gold, when the US de-linked from gold, all currencies were de facto de-linked. *This was the first time in modern history that money was not backed by either gold or silver.*

Momentum alone has carried the global financial system forward since that time, but that time is now over. The fiscally irresponsible spending of the US has now damaged the economic well-being of the US and indeed the world. Out-of-control US fiscal and trade deficits are threatening the very stability of the global financial system.

In June 2006, the head of the International Monetary Fund, Rodrigo de Rato, warned that the US negative trade balance risks plunging the world economy into recession and a monetary crisis.

The risk is that if nothing is done, imbalances will not be reduced gradually, but suddenly, and in a disruptive way.

Rodrigo de Rato warned that if investors suddenly became unwilling to hold US financial assets, the US dollar would plummet and US interest rates would rise, leading to global financial turmoil and a recession.

For two decades, Central Banks had helped the US Federal Reserve in stabilizing currencies by supporting paper money and suppressing gold. This has changed, as it is now understood that US spending and trade imbalances are the major threats to the world economy, not the price of gold.

The alliance of Central Banks supporting paper money against gold has dwindled considerably; but, more importantly, the Central Banks seeking to increase their gold reserves include the Central Banks of China, Russia, and the Middle East, all with large amounts of US dollars looking now to convert those dollars into gold.

The war between paper money and gold is in its last days. If your investments are not now allocated towards gold or like assets, you will soon find yourself on the losing side in a war you did not know was being waged.

IN THIS WAR
THERE WILL BE NO PRISONERS TAKEN
THERE WILL ONLY BE CASUALTIES AND VICTORS

Section IV

SECTION V

THE REAL DEBATE
INFLATION OR DEFLATION
TRAPPED BETWEEN TWO NIGHTMARES

Topic 22

It is in the beginning that the reason for the end can usually be found. When the dot.com bubble burst in 2000, it was deflation that Greenspan feared. Now, interrupted by an intervening property and investment bubble, irrespective of what the pundits say, it is not inflation, but deflation that keeps Central Bankers worrying and awake at night. The nightmare is not yet over. It has not yet even begun.

Prior to 2008/2009, the discussion in financial columns was focused on inflation. The two reasons are: (1) inflation is perceived to be the immediate threat to the economy, determining whether or not interest rates will rise, and (2) the possibility of deflation is so fundamentally threatening, Central Bankers discuss it only in private, out of the public eye. Deflation is the elephant in the room which no one will acknowledge.

In our credit-money system, price inflation is the inevitable consequence of constantly increasing flows of debt. In such a system, expansion is followed by contraction, ad infinitum. As money is but debt-in-motion, over time, debt levels will eventually attain such heights that they can no longer be sustained. At that time the expansion will turn into a contraction commonly referred to as a recession.

A particularly apt description of this expansion/contraction process follows, excerpted from an article titled Ponzi Economy, posted July 10, 2006 at www.dailyreckoning.com.

PONZI ECONOMY

Everybody likes a credit boom. They all believe they have more money. This is the dirty little secret of modern central banking. It only works by stealth and fraud — silently debauching the currency so that people make mistakes.

The businessman believes there is more demand for his products than there really is. The consumer believes he has more purchasing power than he really has. The lender believes the borrower is a better risk than he really is. All these mistaken judgments lead to spending, investing and lending — which look to all the world like a bona-fide boom.

But it is an ersatz boom, a public spectacle, founded on fraud, expanded into farce, and ending ultimately in disaster. Eventually, everyone gets too stretched out on credit.

Then, the bubble finally finds a pin somewhere, and the air wheezes out. That's the part that no one cares for, because it is when people discover that they've made mistakes, that they've over-reached, and that they've been had.

If, as we believe, we're at the beginning of the disaster stage, the Fed's real enemy is not inflation at all; it's deflation. Typically, a credit contraction shrinks everything down with it. Earnings go down. Consumer spending is reduced. GDP growth falls...or even goes negative. And prices for most financial assets dive.

When a deflationary collapse is severe enough—when the preceding bubble is large enough—it becomes a depression. Fortunately, such occurrences are as rare as they are severe. In the 20th century it happened only once, in the aftermath of the 1920s US speculative stock market bubble—until that time, the largest speculative bubble in history.

Two larger bubbles have collapsed since then. The first was the Japanese Nikkei, Japan's stock market in 1990. The second was the US dot.com bubble in 2000. Now a third, the largest in history, is about to deflate.

The third such deflation will be the US and global real estate bubble; the effect of the implosion of these three trillion-dollar bubbles will then culminate in the mother of all deflationary collapses—the time of the vulture.

When the Japanese bubble collapsed in 1990, the Nikkei lost 80 % of its value and drove down the prices of residential and commercial property in the process. This collapse of equity and housing prices subsequently unleashed deflationary forces in Japan still in effect today.

Much like a stubborn and malignant cancer, deflation has been eating away at the Japanese economy ever since its appearance in 1990. In spite of 0 % interest rates from 1999 to mid-2006, statistics compiled by The Economist Magazine show what deflation is still doing in Japan.

COUNTRY	HOUSING PRICES1997-2006
United States	+ 100 %
France	+ 127 %
Australia	+ 132 %
Britain	+ 192 %
Ireland	+ 252 %
South Africa	+ 327 %
Japan	- 32 %

DO YOU STILL WONDER WHY GREENSPAN WORRIED ABOUT A SPECULATIVE BUBBLE FORMING IN THE US?

If deflation occurs in the US, it will be far worse than what happened to Japan. The Japanese economy did not slide into a deflationary depression because during the 1990s, the US economy, in a credit-driven expansion, imported billions of dollars of Japanese products.

The American expansion occurred exactly as the Japanese economy was contracting and because the Japanese economy is export driven, the US expansion kept Japan from slipping down the slope that all Central Bankers fear, the slope that ends in a deflationary depression.

Such will not be the case if the US succumbs to deflationary forces.

The US no longer is an export economy, but is now a very large importer. No longer capable of exporting itself out of deflation, the US is particularly bereft of options as it approaches the time of the vulture.

This is why Greenspan issued his warning in the fall of 1996, warning the US and Congress that irrational exuberance in the markets might lead to dire consequences.

...how do we know when irrational exuberance has unduly escalated asset values, which then become subject to unexpected and prolonged contractions as they have in Japan over the past decade?

Greenspan was warning specifically about deflation and what had occurred in Japan. When the US bubble was allowed to grow until it collapsed in March 2000, US markets began to deflate as Greenspan had predicted forcing the Fed to slash rates in order to stop deflationary forces from turning into a deflationary depression.

What the 1 % interest rates set in motion, however—a multi-trillion dollar real estate bubble—may in fact cause the very deflationary depression Greenspan hoped to avoid; a depression that would affect not only the US, but the entire world.

Beginning October 2006, over 1.4 million adjustable-rate real estate loans worth in excess of $2 trillion were due to be "re-adjusted". The US now has over 5 million adjustable-rate real estate mortgages and 25 % of those loans are now due to be re-adjusted upwards.

It is estimated that monthly mortgage payments on these loans will increase by 50 % or more. An increase of this magnitude will send a significant number of those loans directly into foreclosure.

The deflating real estate bubble will not only cause a wave of foreclosures, it will also wreak havoc on the millions of homeowners who refinanced their homes during the bubble. Since 2001, over one trillion dollars has been extracted from homeowner equity by refinancing.

The problem is that much of that equity was never real; it was only bubble equity temporarily inflated by the availability of low cost loans. Now that loan costs are higher, home prices will drop, as will existing valuations, but the money spent and now owed will remain. Many homeowners will find themselves with negative equity, owing more than their homes are worth.

Many homeowners will choose to walk away rather than make payments in excess of what their homes are worth. If they do, they will then discover they cannot do so easily. Because they refinanced their homes, they will discover that their refinanced mortgages are now categorized as recourse loans, instead of the non-recourse loans they originally were.

A NON-RECOURSE LOAN ALLOWS
THE LENDER TO REPOSSESS THE HOUSE

A RECOURSE LOAN ALLOWS THE LENDER
TO REPOSSESS THE HOUSE AND ATTACH
ALL ASSETS OWNED BY THE DEBTOR

ONLY THE BANKERS WILL HAVE RECOURSE
THE BORROWERS WILL HAVE NONE

When a homeowner has refinanced his home, in case of default the bank can take back the house, but can also attach all wages, bank accounts, cars, etc. This is the position in which many homeowners will soon find themselves.

BUT THE
GREATEST DANGER
IS THAT THE COLLAPSE OF
THE GLOBAL REAL ESTATE BUBBLE
WILL AWAKEN GLOBAL DEFLATIONARY FORCES

A deflationary recession in the US could plunge Japan back into the deflation it has been struggling to overcome since 1990; and with both the US and Japan in the grip of deflationary forces, the world economy will be at risk as never before—at least not since the 1930s.

The above words were written in 2006. Now, in 2012, the threat of deflation is again a threat. The collapse of the housing bubble in 2007/2008 and the collapse of equities in 2008/2009 has brought the world economy to its knees, rekindling dormant deflationary forces in Japan and now in the US and Europe.

The feared consequences of a deflationary collapse in demand followed by falling prices and rising unemployment is no longer a feared prediction. It is a reality. Central bank fears of a deflation collapse have come true. Their nightmare is next. The Time of the Vulture is at hand.

2012 UPDATE: In 2007, deflation, Greenspan's nightmare, was only a fear. Today, it has started and Greenspan's nightmare has now become Bernanke's; and just as Greenspan wondered if he could have prevented the Great Depression (he couldn't as he's now responsible for starting another), Bernanke believed he could keep an economic contraction from turning into a deflationary depression.

But, like Greenspan, Bernanke's self-confidence was greater than his ability. Succeeding Greenspan as Fed chairman in 2007, Bernanke got his chance to put Milton Friedman's theories to the test when Greenspan's property bubble collapsed in 2008

Applying 'Friedman's fix', i.e. his mentor's preferred solution, Bernanke opened the Fed's floodgates in 2009 unleashing an unprecedented flow of credit, hoping to reverse the contraction of the money supply then underway.

Bernanke assumed, as Milton Friedman had taught, that sufficient monetary easing would reverse a monetary contraction and thus prevent another Great Depression. Although Friedman's theory had never been put to the test in real time, Bernanke was sure that his mentor had discovered the solution to the Great Depression. He was wrong.

Deflation is again now threatening the world economy and, today, not only is Japan still trapped in a deflationary cycle,

China, too, is in danger of succumbing as well. On July 9, 2012, Ambrose Evans-Pritchard wrote in The Independent UK:

China is on the cusp of a deflationary vortex... This was signaled late last year by the sharpest contraction in the (real) M1 money supply since modern records began. ...Consumer prices have been falling for the last three months, producer prices have been falling for four months... "the deflationary spiral looks to have started...Persistent deflation can be poisonous," said Xianfang Ren from IHS Global Insight in Beijing... it can be poisonous and China already has the twin-afflictions of the deflation ...

Albert Edwards from Societe Generale said the danger now is that China suddenly lurches into a deeper downturn, unleashing a flood of excess goods onto global markets and sending a powerful deflationary impulse across the world...Large parts of the Atlantic system are already disturbingly close to deflation.

Confirming Albert Edwards' warning about deflation in Europe, only 10 days after The Independent UK warned about deflationary forces in China, the New York Times wrote on July 19, 2012: *IMF warns of "sizable risk" of deflation in euro zone.*

Deflation, the nightmare of central bankers, is back.

VULTURE STRATEGY
WHAT TO BUY
WHEN TO SELL

Topic 23

In times of expansion, it is to the hare the prizes go. Quick, risk taking, and bold, his qualities are exactly suited to the times. In periods of contraction, the tortoise is favored. Slow and conservative, quick only to retract his vulnerable head and neck, his is the wisest bet when the slow and sure is preferable to the quick and easy.

Every so often, however, there comes a time when neither the hare nor the tortoise is the victor. This is when both the bear and the bull have been vanquished. When the pastures upon which the bull once grazed are long gone and the bear's lair itself lies buried deep beneath the rubble of economic collapse.

This is the time of the vulture. For the vulture feeds neither upon the pastures of the bull nor the stored up wealth of the bear. The vulture feeds instead upon the blind ignorance and denial of the ostrich. The time of the vulture is at hand.

When the economic-collapse occurs, a multi-trillion dollar edifice of paper assets—stocks, bonds, derivatives, mortgages, etc. will lie buried beneath a mountain of debt. Many of these assets will be worthless. Some will be valuable. But all, worthless and valuable alike, will be available for pennies on the dollar during the time of the vulture.

The vulture investment strategy is clear and straightforward:

PRIOR TO THE COLLAPSE
INVEST IN GOLD
WHEN THE COLLAPSE OCCURS
GOLD WILL EXPLODE UPWARDS
SELL GOLD
AND BUY
ANYTHING YOUR HEART DESIRES
FOR PENNIES ON THE DOLLAR

While gold is not the only investment to be considered, it will offer the highest returns during the time of the vulture. Because a dramatic loss of confidence in the US dollar and paper money will affect the entire financial system, paper's opposite—gold, will be the haven of choice in such times.

Traditional methods of investing are appropriate in traditional times. The time of the vulture is not a traditional time. It is a unique one-time event. It may have been prudent in times past to diversify investments so as to hedge one's bets against any uncertainty. Today, the times are no longer what they once were and they will soon be what they have never been.

Diversification is a protection against ignorance. It makes very little sense for those who know what they're doing.
- Warren Buffet

There is now only one economic certainty and that is the omega event that lies in front of us. Gold will be the major recipient of this event. There are other investments that will benefit but the simplest and most straightforward approach is to buy gold, hold it until the collapse occurs. Then sell, unless you want to continue to hold gold as a long-term investment.

IN THE TIME OF THE VULTURE
THE PRICE OF GOLD MAY REACH $4,000 TO $5,000

When the collapse happens, the distance between the valuation of gold and the US dollar will be at its most extreme. It is fear that is going to drive this omega event and when it occurs, fear will be at its most extreme.

When it dawns upon the players that the casino itself is in trouble, a frantic stampede to the exits will ensue. Most players, however, will not make it to the door; and for those who do, the cabbies outside will want payment in gold.

Be fearful when others are greedy. Be greedy when others are fearful.
- Warren Buffet

In 2006, the Japanese Central Bank raised its rates for the first time in six years and the markets are unsettled and uncertain; waiting for signals as to whether the bull will resume its upward path or whether the bear will take over where the bull left off.

What the markets do not yet understand is that neither the bull nor the bear will be standing in the days ahead. Both will lie buried deep beneath the rubble of economic collapse as the vulture feeds on what they left behind.

Place your bets only on what is certain. It is certain currencies will fall and gold will rise. As observers watch helplessly, the US budget and trade deficits grow ever larger, now exceeding $2 trillion a year with no apparent end in sight. This gargantuan growing deficit guarantees the collapse of the US dollar and the fall of other currencies. You can bank on it—the only question being, how best to do so.

Investing in high grade non-US dollar denominated foreign government bonds is one way to take advantage of a falling dollar. But because many foreign bond funds hedge against currency risks to protect the original investment, you must choose a bond fund that does not hedge. One such fund is the American Century International Bond Fund, BEGBX.

An article in the Dallas Morning News, January 24, 2005, by Scott Burns discusses how the American Century International Bond Fund specifically profits from a falling US dollar.

> *American Century International Bond (ticker: BEGBX) and T. Rowe Price International Bond are among the very few funds that don't hedge. Both are no-load funds and have minimum investments of $2,500.*
>
> *When the dollar is sinking, you'll enjoy great returns. When the dollar is rising, these funds will do poorly compared with domestic bond funds. Both funds, for instance, had annual losses in 1999, 2000 and 2001. The average intermediate-term domestic bond fund also lost money in 1999 but provided attractive returns in 2000 and 2001.*
>
> *In the 12 months ending Nov. 30, the American Century fund provided a total return of 16.6 percent while the T. Rowe Price fund provided a total return of 14.4 percent.*

KIPLINGER MAGAZINE REPORTED IN MAY 2006 THAT UP TO 25 % OF VICE-PRESIDENT DICK CHENEY'S ASSETS ARE INVESTED IN THE AMERICAN CENTURY INTERNATIONAL BOND FUND

Since Vice President Cheney is apparently banking on a falling US dollar, he might know something you do not. And if you still feel a need to follow those in authority, this is one of the few instances in which you might be rewarded for so doing.

In mid-2008, the US dollar began rising in value as investors bought the dollar when they were forced to exit leveraged trades. Both the US dollar and Yen showed unexpected strength while their economies continued to disintegrate.

The rise of the US dollar and Yen are temporary as are the speculative forces causing their ascent. Someday, those same speculative forces will drive currencies into the dirt as the empires of paper wealth become the graveyard of fiat currencies. Putting faith in paper promises will reap its own inevitable reward.

As the time of the vulture draws near, there will be other ways to take advantage of the coming collapse. Gold, of course, is our first choice. In these most uncertain of times, if you play your cards right at the right table, you *will* profit. But remember:

YOU WILL PROFIT MOST WHEN THE CASINO ITSELF
COLLAPSES

2012 Update: While some estimate gold will reach $5,000, some believe it will go even higher. What is certain is that in the end, all currencies will fall against gold; and, if hyperinflation occurs, the sky's the limit—literally.

HOW HIGH IS UP
HOW FAR IS DOWN
THE DISTANCE IS THE SAME
THE PERSPECTIVE IS NOT

Topic 24

A full or near-full economic collapse is often quickly followed by months, years, or even decades of economic depression, social chaos, and civil unrest...The most obvious of these examples is the 1929 Stock Market Crash...In the 1920s, the widespread use of the home mortgage and credit purchases of automobiles and furniture boosted spending but created consumer debt. People who were deeply in debt when a price deflation occurred were in serious trouble—even if they kept their jobs—and risked default. Indeed, prices and incomes fell 20-50 %, but the debts remained at the same dollar amount. As the debtors tightened their belts, consumer spending fell, and the whole economy weakened. With future profits looking poor, capital investment slowed or stopped. In the face of bad loans and worsening future prospects, banks became more conservative. They built up their reserves, which intensified the deflationary pressures. The downward spiral sped up. This kind of self-aggravating process may have turned a 1930 recession into a 1933 depression.

- Economic Collapse, Wikipedia 2006

How far will the markets drop in the coming economic-collapse? After the 1929 collapse, the US stock market declined 90 %; in 1952, the Dow was still down 75 % from its 1929 high. When the Nikkei collapsed in 1990, it fell 80 %, finally reaching a bottom thirteen years later in 2003. Next time, how far will the markets fall, how long will the torpor persist?

With the Dow Jones over 13,000, an 80 % drop in the Dow would bring the Dow down to 2,600. A 90 % drop would lower the Dow to 1,300 which is still 67 % higher than its last bottom at 777 in 1982. A thirteen year slide to a market bottom would be reached in the year 2020. Is a decline of such magnitude possible today?

Unfortunately, it is not only possible, it is virtually certain. The next bubble is far larger than the 1929 stock market bubble, the 1990 Japanese Nikkei bubble, and the 2000 dot.com bubble; and because the larger the bubble, the farther the fall—the mother of all economic-collapses is now right in front of us.

The worldwide rise in house prices is the biggest bubble in history. Prepare for the pain when it pops.

- The Economist, June 16, 2005

One of the gifts the internet brings is the ability to read periodicals and newspapers from different countries. Then and only then can Americans understand that what they see, read, and hear is strained through a filter, much as baby food is processed for easier consumption. It is uncertain whether Americans really wish to know the truth, what is certain is that they do not receive it.

When the truth is presented, alluded or referred to in America, it is usually crafted in an equivocal manner; scientific fact such as global warming is presented as debatable opinion so as not to offend those in power or those whose advertising dollars support their bottom lines.

While this arrangement is ideally suited for crowd control, it fails to inform the citizenry of the truths they need to know in order to make informed decisions. But, of course, this is not the intent of those who control America—those who believe that important decisions should not be left in the hands of those who vote.

The Economist, published in the UK, is an interesting publication. Professing a belief that free markets bring the greatest benefit to the greatest number of people even while admitting this has not so far worked out, The Economist nonetheless is a fount of observation and information presented in a lively and perceptive manner rarely encountered on this side of the Atlantic.

While it is certainly not always right, it is nonetheless a breath of fresh air to read in America, where the stench of vested interests and money far too often influences what is presented or opined. Money, while being a wonderful thing to spend, is by nature a terrible conductor of truth.

In June 2005, The Economist published an article on the current global housing boom. The article, *In Come the Waves*, noted the following:

> *According to estimates by The Economist, the total value of residential property in developed economies rose by more than $30 trillion over the past five years, to over $70 trillion, an increase equivalent to 100 % of those countries' combined GDPs. Not only does this dwarf any previous house-price boom, it is larger than the global stockmarket bubble in the late 1990s (an increase over five years of 80 % of GDP) or America's stockmarket bubble in the late 1920s (55 % of GDP). In other words, it looks like the*

THE BIGGEST BUBBLE IN HISTORY

Everyone is going to be affected by the collapse of the global real estate bubble, a bubble larger than any that preceded it—and the consequences of the collapse of this bubble will be unprecedented.

Perhaps the closest approximation of what will occur is what happened to real estate values in post-bubble Japan. After the collapse of the Nikkei, prices of residential real estate fell for fourteen years, losing 40 % of their value. Commercial real estate fell even more, losing 80 %. But what is about to happen in the US is going to be far worse than what happened in Japan.

Japan was saved from a deflationary depression only by its ability to maintain high levels of exports during the time its economy contracted and by its high rate of savings, the highest in Asia.

But there will be no safety net of export dollars or savings to help America during the coming economic-collapse. The US can no longer create wealth by trade. Nor do Americans have a cushion of savings as did the Japanese, with which to weather a severe economic downturn.

The Japanese rate of savings, the highest in the world, allowed it to internally finance the extraordinary levels of debt necessary to stay afloat in the midst of severe deflationary pressures. The US, however, has no savings and is the world's largest debtor. In 2005, the US savings rate entered negative territory. The last time this happened was in 1933 during the Great Depression. Now, as the US teeters on the edge of economic-collapse, it needs to borrow $1 trillion each year just in order to continue teetering.

When the real estate bubble began to deflate in 2007, it set in motion the deflation of other asset bubbles; and, now, with the largest bubble in history deflating on the heels of the collapse of the largest stock market bubble in history, the US will succumb to an economic-collapse with deflationary pressures continually forcing real estate and stock prices lower for years, just as they did in Japan in the 1990s.

The difference is that the US will have no way to protect itself from the ravaging onslaught of a full blown collapse as did Japan. With no savings and unable to generate income by trade, the US has only one remaining tool in its economic arsenal: its ability to print paper money.

But if the US turns to printing money to inflate its way out of its financial problems, the value of its increasingly commonplace paper dollars will become increasingly worthless. And when that happens, the flight from the US dollar will begin in earnest.

The above words were written in 2006 when it was not known what the US and other governments would do when global markets collapsed as predicted. Now, in 2009, there is no longer any doubt. The choice has been made.

THE CENTRAL BANKS WILL PRINT AND PRINT AND PRINT THE MONEY

If the current chairman of the US Federal Reserve, "Helicopter" Ben Bernanke, makes good on his threat to run the printing presses non-stop and drop money from helicopters to stimulate demand, runaway inflation will result somewhere in the future leading to hyperinflation.

In response to an ever-worsening economic collapse, governments have instead come to the aid of the banks that themselves caused the problems, not their citizens. This will only prolong the problem and in the end, make matters worse.

Governments are not trying to solve the problems they themselves created. They are trying to save the system by which they and the bankers profit. Systemic collapse can no longer be prevented and the unrestrained printing of money will in the future lead to the collapse of currencies as paper money issued by beleaguered governments becomes increasingly worthless.

How bad will the economic devastation be? If the collapse of the 1929 US and 1990 Japanese bubbles are an indication of what the sequential collapse of the dot.com and housing bubbles will bring—IF YOU DO NOTHING, in a few years your stocks could be worth 10 % to 20 % of their present value and your house worth only 20%-40 % of what it can be sold for today.

If you have a more pleasant future scenario *that is not based on denial,* by all means disbelieve what has been presented here. If, however, your disbelief and denial is based on a refusal to accept what has happened and what might happen, understand that your disbelief and denial will not change by one iota what is to come.

What it will affect is your ability and the ability of your family to survive the coming devastation and the consequences that will soon be upon us.

2012 UPDATE: After presenting my analysis of the US and global economy in 2007, the economic collapse began to happen; Wall Street banks collapsed in 2008 and US real estate prices fell 40%-70%.

Although in mid-2012 the stock market has remained relatively resistant to the collapse, this is due only to the massive injections of liquidity by the Fed. Monetary easing, like steroids, initially will have a 'positive' effect; but, like steroids, when usage is prolonged, the consequences are fatal. The collapse of all paper markets is just a matter of time—and time is running out.

WHO WILL SKATE WHO WILL FALL
WHO WILL PAY FOR THE SINS OF ALL

Topic 25

No one enjoys being subject to the rule of law, least of all those who make them.

To the unknowing, which includes myself, S.I. refers to Sports Illustrated, a magazine best known for its in-depth coverage of sports and its annual swimsuit competition.

To the cognoscenti, however, S.I. refers to the long-running and much-beloved Style Invitational, an extraordinary and wonderful weekly contest sponsored by the Washington Post newspaper.

Wikipedia describes the genesis of the Washington Post Style Invitational as follows:

> *The Style Invitational kicked off in March 1993 by asking readers to come up with a less offensive name for the Washington Redskins. The winner, published two weeks later, was Douglas R. Miller, with the entry:*
>
> *"The Baltimore Redskins. No, don't move the team, just let Baltimore deal with it"*

What warrants our attention, however, is the 2003 Style Invitational contest, which asked entrants to take any word from the dictionary, alter it by adding, subtracting, or changing one letter, and supply a new definition.

Among the winners was the following entry:

> *Intaxication: Euphoria at getting a tax refund, which lasts until you realize it was your money to start with.*

But the one most relevant to our topic at hand is:

CASHTRATION

Cashtration (n.): The act of buying a house, which renders the subject financially impotent for an indefinite period.

Cashtration, in fact, perfectly describes the condition of those who purchased or refinanced homes during the recent housing bubble. Those who did so early in the cycle will be far more fortunate than those who did so later. All, however, will suffer for having done so.

When housing prices falter in 2007 and 2008 and the years that follow, as they always do after the collapse of large speculative bubbles, the carnage will be immense and widespread.

It may be argued (and it surely will) that a fall in real estate valuations did not occur after the collapse of the dot.com bubble in 2000, so why should it now? The argument, however, is as fatuous as it is false.

The reason that real estate prices did not fall in 2001 is that the US Federal Reserve quickly slashed interest rates to 1 % and turned the spigot of credit into a veritable floodgate of cheap mortgages to prevent the inevitable crash in real estate from then occurring.

However, a crash postponed is not a crash averted, and the sudden appearance of low cost loans, made instantly available to those who could otherwise not afford them, had the immediate effect of setting in motion a housing bubble of unprecedented magnitude.

This began a speculative frenzy which drove housing prices to unheard of valuations in such a short period that the memory of the preceding dot.com bubble was soon eclipsed by a new wealth paradigm where instead of a computer science degree from MIT, qualifying for a no-money down payment adjustable-rate mortgage would now suffice.

The new high valuations were turned into instant cash by the easy availability of refinancing options. In this way alone, over one trillion dollars was borrowed and spent, as consumers did more than their share in keeping the economy afloat.

Now, however, the money's spent and gone but still owed and the party is winding down along with the prices of the overvalued properties. Those who purchased or refinanced homes do not yet realize that they have been trapped into paying for properties that will soon decline in value.

In the coming economic-collapse, real estate prices will most likely fall by 40 % or more (as they already have in 2009). But while prices will fall, the mortgages on those properties will not. In fact, if the mortgages are adjustable-rate mortgages, payments will increase as property values drop.

In a most perceptive article on what happened during the recent property bubble, Michael Hudson wrote in *The New Road to Serfdom: An Illustrated Guide to the Coming Real Estate Collapse*, Harper's magazine, May 2006:

> *...this particular real estate bubble has been carefully engineered to lure home buyers into circumstances detrimental to their own best interests. The bait is easy money. The trap is a modern equivalent to peonage, a lifetime spent working to pay off debt on an asset of rapidly dwindling value...A real estate boom that began with the promise of "economic freedom" will almost certainly end with a growing number of workers locked into a lifetime of debt servitude that absorbs every spare penny.*

As troubling as this is, what is truly disturbing is what the "carefully engineered" housing bubble made possible. As middle-class families pressed for cash refinanced their homes and as others took "advantage" of never before available low cost mortgages to buy homes they could otherwise not afford—the wealthy used the housing bubble as an opportunity to run the table one last time, grabbing as much as they could before the US descended into a full blown economic-collapse.

CREDIT APPLICATION

> **2012 Update:** The collapse of the US housing bubble in 2007/2008 destabilized all remaining housing bubbles around the world, e.g. Spain, Canada, Australia and China. Housing was capitalism's greatest bubble; and the collapse of its largest remaining bubble, China's housing market, may bring down the bankers' entire house of cards.

SECTION VI

THE FOX IS IN THE HENHOUSE
THE CHICKENS IN DISARRAY
BANKERS RUN THE COUNTRY
THE PEOPLE HAVE NO SAY

Topic 26

You have a choice between the natural stability of gold and the honesty and intelligence of the members of government. And with all due respect for those gentlemen, I advise you, as long as the capitalist system lasts, vote for gold.

- George Bernard Shaw

It is easy to tell if an establishment is prosperous and expanding. The management is doing a good job, the company's books are in order, capital is allocated towards growth, debt is minimal, and customer satisfaction would be high.

It is also easy to tell if a business is failing. Management would be giving themselves large raises and undeserved bonuses. Debt would be disproportionate to profits. Customers would be treated badly because management knows its days are numbered and its first concern is to take care of itself before the business shuts down for good.

So, too, it is with government. If a government is well run, its books are in order and those governed are satisfied with those who govern. As far as the US and its books being in order, in its July/August 2006 *Review*, the St Louis Federal Reserve Bank published a report by Professor Laurence Kotlikoff stating that:

The gap between future US receipts and future US government obligations now totals $65.9 trillion, a sum that is impossible for the US to reconcile, which means the US is now technically bankrupt.

In publishing Kotlikoff's report, the St Louis Federal Reserve Bank attempted to draw public attention to the dangerous state of the US economy, a topic which then President, George W. Bush, assiduously avoided.

The President's avoidance was not accidental. It was deliberate and occurred because the President was busy helping the rich and well-connected loot the country of any remaining assets before the roof caves in. Perhaps this may help unsuspecting Americans understand why the President and Congress remain unresponsive to their concerns.

Insofar as trusting Congress and the President, the numbers are in.

	Americans
Low respect for the President	69 %
Low respect for Congress	76 %
Do not trust government	63 %

Recently in America, however, politicians have found a new and more effective way to insulate themselves from voter dissatisfaction—electronic voting machines.

WITH NO SAFEGUARDS TO VERIFY ITS VOTES
THE US IS NOW THE WORLD'S LARGEST DEMOCKERY

Americans have played follow the leader for years. In so doing, they have been played for fools. The game will not, however, be played much longer.

Fooling people is harder when they're broke and out of a job. 2008, the year of the next presidential election, promises to be very interesting. Provided, of course, the voting machines are not fixed come election time.

I'm the decider and I decide what's best.
                                            - President George W. Bush

President George W. Bush Jr. was not the "decider" he claimed to be. That job was already taken and belonged to Vice-President Dick Cheney. Ex-President Bush was actually the "fooler", the man whose job it is to fool Americans. And as the fooler, he did a very good job; certainly a far better job than Cheney has done as the decider.

> *See, in my line of work you got to keep repeating things over and over and over again for the truth to sink in, to kind of catapult the propaganda.*
>
> - President George W. Bush

When the dot.com bubble burst in March 2000, the deflationary pressures that plagued Japan immediately surfaced in the US, and US stock markets began to decline rapidly. In just two years, the NASDAQ had lost 80 % of its value, the Dow lost 36 %, and the S&P suffered a 45 % decline.

Something had to be done and it was. Unfortunately, President Bush and Congress acted not to save the country and its citizens. They acted to save the net worth of the richest and best able to weather an economic downturn. The government came to the aid of the rich and well-connected, and the middle-class and the poor are now about to bear the brunt of what the government has done.

As the country's fortunes fell, the US government gave the rich a huge tax cut and inflated a new bubble by extending massive amounts of credit to those who could not before qualify then tightened US bankruptcy laws to ensure that those they trapped will be forever indebted to the bankers who are benefiting as never before.

The collapse of the housing bubble in 2006/2007 and the stock bubble in 2008 caused Americans to finally vote out the Republicans under whose aegis much of the economic destruction was crafted and carried out.

First Bendover Bank & Trust Co.

WE MAKE MONEY ON THE SPREAD

In the fall of 2008, America was returned to the control of Democrats who themselves set in motion much of the economic suffering that will now occur. In 1999, under Democrat Bill Clinton, the US repealed the Glass-Steagall Act passed in 1932 to prevent another depression.

The economic consequences that will now bring this once great nation to its knees was set in motion by both Democrats and Republicans who put their political futures ahead of the future of the nation.

THOUGHT THEY WOULDN'T?

When the story is written after the collapse, it will become clear what went amiss and who was responsible. Now, however, as the collapse unfolds, it is clear that both parties sold out the nation and the nation will pay for the sins of those they elected to lead them.

Credit was the means by which bankers corrupted the nation. Easy credit at the trough of government largesse is what set in motion the terrors of tomorrow. Easy credit has often been compared to heroin.

At first, it feels good, so good that everyone wants more. As with heroin, however, easy credit always brings with it a day of reckoning and that day is coming very, very soon.

IN THE NOT TOO DISTANT FUTURE COLD TURKEY WILL BE THE MAIN DISH ON AMERICA'S TABLES

2012 UPDATE: The economic collapse was so extreme that, in 2008, Americans voted overwhelming for change; and, for the first time in history, they elected a black man to be president of the United States.

Unfortunately, during his first term in office Barack Obama resembled more his white predecessors than the substantive change most Americans wanted. During Obama's first term, the bankers who were responsible for the economic collapse continued to receive government favors and the collusive and corrosive sweetheart deals between Washington DC and Wall Street continued.

The close relationship between Wall Street banks and the Democrats—a relationship to be expected with Republicans— was a carry-over from the Clinton years when Bill Clinton sold out his constituency for his own political ambitions; for it was during Clinton's presidency when Wall Street bankers made gains impossible under a Republican president.

Clinton gave the Republicans what they already hadn't achieved under Reagan. His administration allowed Rupert Murdoch and Fox News access to America. Clinton also signed America's economic death warrant by allowing China into the WTO, resulting in the export of America's jobs, and repealed the Glass-Steagall Act, allowing Wall Street bankers to bet the savings of Americans, a practice outlawed in the Great Depression. Three out of three, the Republicans couldn't have done better with one of their own.

Politicians in both parties are now bought and paid for by

America's economic elite. Expecting politicians to protect us against the predatory policies of those who own them is absurd. The two-party system has divided Americans one against the other and has rendered the nation incapable of agreeing on what needs to be done.

God save America. It's clear Americans are incapable of saving themselves.

AMBITION AND GREED
THOSE IN CONTROL
UPON US THEY FEED

Topic 27

If you seek to understand the world of human activity, look first to the self-interests of those involved. As true for the whole as it is for the parts, you will by so doing come to understand the actions of nations as well as the behavior of individual men and women. And when you do discover what the underlying self-interests are, you will discover too the actual nature of the self then being served.

- Light in a Dark Place, 2nd Edition

The owners of the USS US, those who control the destiny of the nation, have at their disposal the brightest and most willing to serve the needs of whoever pays them. Alan Greenspan is very smart. He understands intellectually and intuitively the context and consequences of monetary policy. He also understands on which side his bread is buttered and who butters it.

Greenspan's warning to the Congress about the dangers of allowing a financial bubble to grow was ignored and over-ridden by those who control our country. Although Greenspan knew full well the consequences of allowing the stock market bubble to grow, Alan's ambition dictated that Alan Greenspan KBE serve those who paid him.

When Greenspan's warning about the financial bubble was shunned by those in power, Greenspan's public policy pronouncements turned on a dime and so did the destiny of America. No matter how knowledgeable those in control, no matter how many scenarios they commission and study, in the end their decisions are driven by ambition and greed.

It was ambition that caused the military-industrial complex and their corporate colleagues to spend all and more of America's gold after WWII. And it was greed that caused the bankers on Wall Street to have their minions in Washington DC rein in Alan Greenspan in 1996.

IT IS BECAUSE OF AMBITION AND GREED MANY OF THOSE WHO CONTROL OUR NATION ACHIEVED THEIR CURRENT POSITIONS TO DO SO

Not all politicians, not all in the military-industrial complex, not all in the corporate world are so corrupted, but many are. If a few bad apples will spoil a barrel, it does not take much imagination to see what a few more will do.

A FEW BAD APPLES AND MORE

One only has to look at America today. At one time the envy of the world, America is now feared and distrusted, not admired and respected. Once the freest nation on earth, now the tyrannies of the Patriot Act substitute for the freedoms formerly guaranteed by the Constitution and Bill of Rights; and once the wealthiest nation in the world, America is now its greatest spendthrift and debtor.

This state of affairs did not happen overnight or by accident. Edwards Deming, the man whose theories catapulted Japan into the forefront of economic power, postulated that when things go amiss or awry, it is not the fault of people, it's the system that's the cause.

A good system will produce good results. A bad system will produce bad results. When a good system goes bad, the reasons must be found and rectified before it will right itself.

It took but a few decades to cause the unfortunate state of affairs America now is in; and it will take some time to determine how to return the country to that which once made it great. The righting of America, the USS US, however, is not the purpose of this analysis.

There will be enough time in the future for that to be accomplished; if in fact, that is to be done. Our purpose now is to explore the various means by which we may individually survive and prosper in the coming days, a time we call the Time of the Vulture.

SO MANY CHOICES
SO LITTLE TIME
GOLD IS THE HAVEN
THE LUCKY WILL FIND

Topic 28

Gold, the most stable in value, the most volatile in price

Until recently, buying and owning gold was difficult except for the wealthy. If you were very wealthy and decided to increase your investments in precious metals, you would call your banker at UBS, the United Bank of Switzerland, inform him of your wish and it would be done, just like that.

Sometimes the "just like that" aspect is all that separates us from those whose desires and whims appear to be so easily satisfied. Well, for those who want to invest in gold "just like that", it just got a whole lot easier.

Exchange-traded funds, ETFs, are an increasingly popular investment vehicle in world stock markets. In the US, SPDR Gold Shares, GLD, a gold ETF, allows investors to directly track the price of gold. When the price of gold rises or falls, the price of a gold ETF does also.

The amount of physical gold held by ETFs has increased from 555 tons in 2007 to almost 1400 tons in 2009, far higher than the gold reserves of many countries. Given what we know about the officially-sanctioned figure fudging of the IMF, the ETFs actual ranking is probably much higher as the published gold reserves of many nations are in fact false.

The growing popularity of gold ETFs is due to the ease with which ETFs allow investors to participate in gold's rise. And as we approach the *TIME OF THE VULTURE,* however, the ease of gold ETFs, such as GLD, is offset by the fact that such ETFs can invest in "paper gold" as well as physical gold.

For those more comfortable with physical possession of gold—either coins or bullion or gold bullion held on deposit—see addendum I in the appendix which includes some of these services.

Price movements of gold can be volatile and will become more so as we approach the Time of the Vulture, though no more so than technology or biotech stocks. This does not mean that gold is always volatile, but that it can be. It must be understood why this is so before you invest in gold.

GOLD IS VOLATILE WHEN CONDITIONS ARE VOLATILE
GOLD IS STABLE WHEN CONDITIONS ARE STABLE

That's it, plain and simple—the more chaotic the monetary conditions, the more chaotic the price of gold. Gold is a barometer of economic uncertainty. In times when inflation threatens, gold moves up and down. In times when deflation threatens, gold moves up and down. When both inflation and deflation threaten, gold moves rapidly up and down.

BECAUSE OF GOLD'S INCREASING VOLATILITY
KNOWING WHEN TO BUY AND WHEN TO SELL
IS THE KEY TO DOING WELL

Prior to economic-collapse, the price of gold will become more and more volatile. Extreme upswings may be followed by brutal corrections in increasingly shorter periods of time. Because of this, it is imperative you have experienced guidance to help with investment decisions. In the addenda that follows, websites are listed offering investment advice and information.

IN TIMES OF MONETARY INSTABILITY
THERE IS NO BETTER INVESTMENT THAN GOLD

Monetary instability does not occur during normal cycles of economic expansion and contraction. Monetary instability occurs only in periods of severe systemic distress. Gold, being the monetary opposite of paper currencies, reacts whenever monetary disequilibrium occurs for any reason, whether inflation, deflation, runaway inflation or deflationary depression.

Because the current monetary disequilibrium is so extreme, so too will be the rise in the price of gold. The possibilities are no longer merely inflation or deflation; the options now include runaway inflation and deflationary depression together in sequence. The time of the vulture is truly at hand.

2012 UPDATE: Previously, SPDR Gold Shares, GLD, the gold ETF, was a convenient way for Americans to profit from gold's rising price. Today, there is a far more important consideration to take into account, *to wit*, GLD will be no guarantee of safety when the final collapse occurs. This is because GLD also invests in "paper gold", e.g. derivatives, and in the end game, only gold bullion will be safe.

GLD and all ETFs that invest in paper gold should be avoided. An additional consideration is that the trust that operates GLD is neither required by its charter to be insured or is it liable for loss, damage, theft, or fraud.

Given these caveats and the track record of the large banks associated with GLD, e.g. Goldman Sachs, Citi, JPMorgan Chase, Bank of America, etc., the problems of GLD more than outweigh its benefits; because the banks associated with GLD are the very banks that have colluded against the rising price of gold.

The end game is the final resolution that will culminate in the

---

flight out of paper assets into gold. Be prepared. Be invested in gold, not GLD or in other forms of paper gold. The end game is near.

WHAT THE TARNATION HYPERINFLATION OR IS THE PROGRESSION DEFLATIONARY DEPRESSION

Topic 29

...it is only a matter of time before something pops -- and the sustainable disequilibrium quickly becomes unsustainable. Given the overhang of excess dollar holdings by poor countries, the flight out of dollars could be fast and furious. That could trigger the dreaded dollar-crash scenario and a related spike in real long-term US interest rates.

- Stephen Roach, Morgan Stanley

Stephen Roach, Managing Director and Chief Economist at Morgan Stanley, the large US investment firm (now a commercial bank after investment banking collapsed in 2008), must be a very patient man. He is like the school principal who, noticing the increasing obesity of his students, sends notes home to the parents every year, warning them that this trend will result in serious health consequences if allowed to continue.

But the parents do nothing, perhaps thinking the concerns of the principal are overblown, that he has been sending them such notes for years and, as yet, none of their children have diabetes, although their doctor recently suggested they should encourage their children to exercise a bit and go easy on the soft drinks.

Highly respected among his peers—a rather high-octane crowd of the world's financial elite—Stephen Roach was nonetheless a distinct minority in the well-heeled and well-oiled crowd which pays for his commentary.

He described what is about to happen as the end-game, the resolution of extreme trade and monetary imbalances that will ultimately destabilize the global financial system and perhaps bring down the entire house of cards. But, like the parents of the increasingly overweight children, the leaders of the world financial community listened but did nothing about Stephen Roach's warnings.

Like alcoholics in denial of the damage being done to their livers, the world's financial elites kept hoping against hope that Stephen Roach was wrong, that the party built on paper money wouldn't end, that their worlds of wealth and ease would continue as usual, that somehow a solution would be discovered, a solution that would bring about a soft instead of a hard landing, a landing which would lay the groundwork for yet another rising market that would again increase the net worth of their investments ten-fold as happened so often in the past.

The elites were wrong, however. The world's experiment with debt-based paper money is now ending. Just as many of the now obese children would go on to develop diabetes, so too have the financial markets now buckled under the strain of unprecedented and unsustainable levels of debt and increasing monetary and trade imbalances. That day, warned of by Stephen Roach, has now arrived.

THE US AND JAPANESE CENTRAL BANKS WILL CONTINUE TO FLOOD THE WORLD WITH INCREASING AMOUNTS OF DEBT-MONEY BECAUSE ANY SLOWDOWN WILL BRING THE HOUSE OF CARDS TUMBLING DOWN

When the world's financial markets buckled in May 2006, the Japanese Central Bank was forced to reverse course and for the first time in fourteen months deposited, not withdrew money, into Japanese banks in order to increase liquidity, i.e. access to debt.

The US and Japan may be raising interest rates but they are still flooding the markets with money and debt because they can no longer choose to do otherwise. Adding additional debt however will only insure the end, not the continuation of the present monetary system.

We are witness to the end of a system, not a temporary problem that will solve itself or be fixed by those in control—because Central Banks are not in control. For those who have staked their hopes and financial futures on the belief that Central Bankers are capable of dealing with what is now happening, be aware that the tail is now wagging the dog.

The situation is so extreme that Central Bankers are being forced to go from crisis to crisis just to keep the global monetary system from collapsing now rather than later.

WHEN PAYMENTS ARE MADE
WITH PROMISES TO PAY
THE END IS NEAR
WOULDN'T YOU SAY

The Central Bank experiment combining a fractional reserve banking system with fiat money is nearing its end. While this is news to those who don't know that paper money is more paper than money, one Central Banker knew exactly what it was and what was going to happen.

That Central Banker was John Exter. In 1939, John Exter entered Harvard graduate school. He wanted to know the reasons for the Great Depression, and there he found his answers.

Exter later attended MIT, worked for the Federal Reserve Board as an economist, and was a Division Chief for the World Bank. His credentials as a Central Banker were impeccable. In 1950, Exter was appointed Governor of the Central Bank of Ceylon (now Sri Lanka).

In 1953 Exter worked for the World Bank as Division Chief for the Middle East and in 1954 was appointed Vice-President in charge of international banking and gold and silver at the Federal Reserve Bank of New York. In 1960 John Exter became Vice President at what is now Citigroup, with special responsibilities for relations with foreign Central Banks and governments.

Like Morgan Stanley's Stephen Roach, John Exter was a member of the moneyed establishment, the ruling elite, the financial cognoscenti who understand the importance of currency flows and the difference between cash and credit. What set Exter apart from his peers, however, was Exter's certainty that our experiment with a fractional reserve banking system and fiat money would end badly.

Exter, the consummate Central Banker, referred to the US dollar and money as "IOU-nothing" money. While inflation might well be interrupted by runaway inflation before deflation arrives, John Exter believed a deflationary collapse was an outcome everyone could bank on.

Exter's prediction is now about to come true. The inflation of the money supply is now so large that money is measured in trillions, because paper is cheap and dollars are so easy to print.

Current US obligations are so overwhelming that the US is technically bankrupt. It is the collapse of this mountain of debt that will usher in the time of the vulture, the deflationary end-game of IOU-nothing money.

US DEFICITS ARE WORSE THAN REPORTED

On August 2, 2006 USA Today reported that the US government keeps two sets of books. Whereas the "official" US deficit in 2005 was reported to be $318 billion, the actual deficit, as determined by standard accounting rules, was $760 billion. If Social Security and Medicare are included, the deficit would actually be $3.5 trillion.

The future will even be worse. The Congressional Budget Office has projected the US deficit will total $1.76 trillion over the next ten years AND if current tax cuts are made permanent the deficit will total $3.26 trillion.

These figures were calculated using "government accounting rules". If standard rules of accounting were applied, the deficit would be double and if Social Security and Medicare were added, well, you add it up if you can.

There's no way all this debt can ever be paid off or even carried by stable economic systems. Forget that. This debt must be carried, handled, by ever increasing amounts of paper.

- Richard Russell, Dow Theory Letters

At some point, the US may start running the printing presses to pay its bills. Indeed, it may have already begun to do so. The decision by the US Federal Reserve to discontinue reporting the total US money aggregate, M3, in March 2006 may have been done to camouflage such printing. The situation is now so extreme, extreme measures will be invoked.

It would do us well to remember the words of Bill Gross, Managing Director of the PIMCO Bond fund:

...the way a reserve currency nation gets out from under the burden of excessive liabilities is to inflate, devalue, and tax.

If the US rapidly inflates the money supply to devalue its current debt and future obligations, such an inflation of the money supply could lead to hyperinflation. This would be hyperinflation in the world's largest economy. If the US runs the printing presses to inflate its way out of debt, a hyperinflation in the US would take down the global financial system.

The United States has experienced high rates of inflation in the past and appears to be running the same type of fiscal policies that engendered hyperinflations in 20 countries over the past century.

-Laurance Kotlikoff, Federal Reserve Bank, *Review*, St Louis, July/Aug 2006

Hyperinflation is no longer a far-fetched possibility. The current chairman of the US Federal Reserve, "Helicopter" Ben Bernanke, received his nickname when he once threatened to run the printing presses and drop money from helicopters to stimulate demand. And if Chairman Bernanke, now the man with his finger on the printing presses, does make good on his threat, the US dollar will be worth the paper its printed on and not much more.

This however is not our decision. It is Mr. Bernanke's, and what he decides to do will affect us all. We do not have a say in the matter. None of our opinions about what should be done will influence what he will do. Mr. Bernanke answers to the President who answers to Wall Street, not to us.

Our responsibility, however, is very clear, our choice simple,

WILL WE PLAY THE OSTRICH OR VULTURE
PLACE YOUR BET NOW
PAPER OR GOLD?

A GOLD MINE IS
NOT A GOLD MINE
WHEN BARRICK IS ITS NAME

Topic 30

For the great majority of mankind are satisfied with appearances, as though they were realities, and are often more influenced by the things that seem than by those that are.

- Niccolò Machiavelli

Prior to gold ETFs, the easiest way for Americans to invest in gold was to buy shares of gold mining companies. During the Great Depression when the Dow lost 90 % of its value, investing in gold mining companies was the only way Americans could protect themselves from the deflationary erosion of their assets.

From a post-1929 low of $7.00 per share, Homestake Mines rose to $68.00 in 1936. The shares of Dome, another gold mining company, went from $6 to $61 plus paid dividends of $16.60 for a total return of 1,293 % during the depression.

In the coming deflationary collapse, gold and gold mining companies will again provide protection and profit in the chaotic days ahead. But not all gold mining companies will do so. The shares of two large gold mining companies, in fact, should be avoided—Barrick Gold and AngloGold Ashanti.

BARRICK GOLD
CAUGHT BY ITS SHORTS
THE LARGEST TRADING LOSS IN HISTORY

Both Barrick Gold and AngloGold Ashanti have pre-sold millions of ounces of gold that are still in the ground to be delivered at now below-market prices. Both Barrick Gold and AngloGold Ashanti have forward-sold so much gold, their selling (1) forced down the price of gold, and (2) it obligated them to deliver gold at below-market prices. And, as the price of gold rises, so too will their losses, already in the billions of dollars.

The excuse of management is that forward-selling allowed Barrick and AngloGold Ashanti to prosper during times of low gold prices. On the surface, this might appear to be true. But, down below where gold is actually mined, another less justifiable reason surfaces.

The massive forward selling of gold by Barrick and AngloGold Ashanti had an enormous downward effect on the price of gold. Many believe that this was the actual, intended, result of two of the largest gold mining companies in the world, a result aligned with the Central Banks' war on gold.

Observers and shareholders alike watched in disbelief as the massive forward-selling (known in the industry as hedging or shorting) by Barrick and AngloGold Ashanti drove down the price of the very product they were mining.

The thoughts of Theodore Butler, a well-respected analyst, are especially revealing regarding the losses at Barrick:

> *What makes the Barrick record derivatives trading loss even more shocking and remarkable is that the company was given ample time and repeated warnings about its outsized gold short position. I know this to be true because I personally warned them. Actually, I did a lot more than warn the company personally; I also warned them publicly. And I did it when gold was below $275 an ounce. In addition, I also contacted and warned their auditors, the New York Stock Exchange (where Barrick trades as ABX), the US Securities and Exchange Commission (SEC) and the Commodity Futures Trading Commission (CFTC).*

135

My main reason for attacking Barrick's short position then was because I felt it was manipulative to gold (and silver) prices. I still do. I know Barrick denies it has manipulated the gold market, but when they put the position on and caused millions of ounces of gold to be dumped on the market, the price of gold dropped by almost $200 an ounce, and when they stopped, the price rose $200. It's as simple as that.

One Barrick shareholder in particular was more than dismayed by what Barrick was doing. The shareholder was Dr. Antal Fekete, who has recently emerged as one of the pre-eminent experts on the relationships between gold, money, and the financial markets.

Dr. Fekete's story was posted on the internet in answer to a question about purchasing shares of Barrick Gold.

TO BARRICK TO BE BARRICKED, THAT IS THE QUESTION

Posted Sunday, 13 August 2006
Antal E. Fekete, former shareholder of Barrick Gold
E-mail: aefekete@hotmail.com

Dear Mr. Kingston:

Thank you for writing. You ask me whether Barrick is a 'buy' now that it has reached its long-time ambition of becoming the first: the largest gold producer of the world. Would it now start moving up from its place of being the last: the world's worst large-cap share price-performer in the gold-mining business?

I am a monetary economist and as a rule do not offer investment advice. Having said that, the name "Barrick" touches a raw nerve in me. I used to be a shareholder. In 1992 I took early retirement from my professorship, accepting bribe money (they call it 'golden handshake') from Memorial University of Newfoundland, my academic home for 35 years. At stake was about $50,000 which I invested in Barrick shares and leaps, with the idea of arbitraging one against the other. As the gold price went up, I would sell leaps and put the proceeds into shares, and vice versa. Most of this investment has gone up in smoke as a result of Barrick's 'Brave New World of

Hedging'. I decided that, in reply to your kind letter, I would tell my story.

The Godfather

Barrick's founder and godfather, Peter Munk, like myself, grew up in Budapest. Truncating the original 'Munkácsy', a name his family shared with one of the most famous Hungarian painters Mihály Munkácsy, Munk got himself a new name when he landed in the New World. We did not know each other but, as schoolboys we had the same experiences, spoke the same street jargon, and trod on the same cobblestones. Above all, gold loomed large in our lives, making an indelible impression. In 1944 Munk's father bought their exit visas from German-occupied Hungary to neutral Switzerland, along with a train-load of other Jews, all paying for their escape with gold. The Swiss government agreed to play the role of go-between.

I learned about the life-saving properties of gold a few months later in a different context. When the Red Army placed Budapest under a siege those who had gold ate; those who didn't went hungry. My family did not have much gold, but there was a heavy gold chain that used to hold the gold pocket watch of my grandfather in better days. The watch itself had been bartered away in hard times for food before I was born during the hyperinflation following World War I. During the next hyperinflation, following World War II, dentists refused to take paper money for professional services rendered. My mother paid for dental work needed by my sister in gold. I still remember the dentist's delicate hands: he clipped off an agreed length of the chain. And his face: he had the smile of Shylock as he was preparing to take his pound of flesh. My mother gave me the remnants of that gold chain, thus abridged, before she died. My wife has it now. It has been fashioned into a pretty bracelet.

Munk came to Canada to study electrical engineering at the University of Toronto. During the pre-Christmas shopping seasons, as a student he was arbitraging Xmas trees between the parking lots of various supermarkets. When I came to

Canada in 1957 I already had my university degree and settled down to a teaching career in Newfoundland. Munk as an electrical engineer went into producing high-end stereo systems and met his first Waterloo in Nova Scotia. He had made the bad decision of accepting government financing for his factory. 'Never again!' he vowed after his business deal with the provincial government unraveled and he lost his entire investment. (This did not prevent him, years later, from courting retired politicians such as former Prime Minister Brian Mulroney of Canada, and Ex-President George Bush, both of whom took their seats on the 'Advisory Board' of Barrick.) The next bad decision was to design luxury hotels (never actually built) in the shadow of the Egyptian pyramids, an idea about as brilliant as setting up a pork-chop stand in Jerusalem.

A little bit of etymology

Munk initially conceived American Barrick in 1980 as a junior oil and gas company. In 1983 he reconstituted it as a gold mining company, renaming it Barrick Gold. I have an avid curiosity about the origin of words and I could not resist the urge to research the word 'Barrick'.

At an early brain-storming session, as described in the authorized biography of Munk, the question was raised how to name the fledgling company. Munk, who was obsessed with big and quick success had no patience with such trivial details, exclaimed: 'Call it Baszik, Szarik, Barrick, as you will; I couldn't care less'. The name Barrick stuck. Knowledge of the Hungarian language helps the etymologist. The first two words' English equivalents are 'f...ck' and 'sh...t'. In Hungarian four-letter words have six letters to sport and, as verbs, they are also distinguished by their '-ik' ending, forming a special conjugation class of their own.

Gold mining and hedging: killing the goose laying the golden egg?

As a shareholder I was concerned about Barrick's preposterous ideas on hedging. Munk was fond of using innovative financing techniques and Barrick boasted that its credit standing is second to none, due to its unique hedging policy. I realized that the word 'hedging' as used by Barrick was a misnomer. It is not hedging at all, any more than a shill is winner at the poker table. The appearance is that she is winning big; in fact she has to surrender every cent of those gains to the casino owner at the end of the day. Barrick was simply selling its production forward, at one point as far as five years out as measured by current output, with settlement postponed, at the option of the 'hedger', for as long as fifteen years. Imagine, no margin calls for fifteen years, no matter how much the price may move against your position! Barrick justified this insane policy by the statistical Principle of Mean Reversal, asserting that all economic indicators, including prices (however volatile) ultimately tend to return to the mean. Fifteen years was considered sufficiently long for even the most 'absurd' spikes in the gold price 'to correct'. I demurred. Gold was an exception to mean reversal. In a hyperinflation, after the 'dead cat bounce' of paper money, you could wait till doomsday for the gold price to correct.

I wrote a paper with the title Gold mining and hedging: killing the goose laying the golden egg? In it I explained that forward selling must be carefully distinguished from hedging. A proper hedging strategy would require that the mine channel production into a fund, which would then buy gold in the open market when the price was low and falling, and sell when the price was high and rising. The income from this arbitrage would more than make up for lost revenues from the outright sale of mine product. Above all, such a strategy would not impart a bearish sentiment to the market. Speculators knew that the gold mine would sooner or later step in as a buyer whenever the gold price weakened, and they would try to preempt it. They would want to buy first. And conversely. The chips could fall where they may.

But since Barrick had an established policy of selling forward, and never buying forward, speculators would abandon the long side of the market in droves. They would move to the short side en bloc, in trying to forestall Barrick. They would want to sell first. Under these circumstances the chips could no longer fall where they may. Fall they did alright, together with gold. The gold price was effectively capped. Worse still was the long-term effect. Just as you cannot 'cap' an active volcano, you can't cap the gold price forever either. It is bound to erupt and, when it does, you can kiss good-bye to the Principle of Mean Reversal. In the end Barrick could be saddled with a king-size liability that it may never be able to live down.

Shareholders do not need to have a PhD in vulcanology to find this out. As soon as they do, they will vote with their feet.

Shareholder-proofing corporate governance

Indeed, they have no alternative. After the Nova Scotia fiasco Munk decided that he would construct a corporate structure that would be 'shareholder-proof'. He developed the 'perfect poison pill'. Not only will Barrick never be the victim of a hostile take-over bid, shareholders will have to eat from his hands. The corporate governance of Barrick epitomizes this. Shareholders are pariahs, sacrificial lambs on the altar of high management policy. They have the right to vote with management. But that's about all. In case of a disagreement they can go and fly a kite. Management lives in its own world of an unassailable bunker.

In 1994 I did not know this. I was naive. I wrote a letter to Munk asking him for a meeting. I wanted to present to him a copy of my paper with my compliments. In reply Munk told me that I had to show my paper to his Senior Vice-President and CFO, Jamie Sokalsky, first. By the time I could see Jamie company headquarters were moved from Yorkville, a bohemian district of Toronto, to the Royal Bank Towers downtown, projecting an entirely different corporate image. The significance of this move was lost on me at the time. I believed that I could convince Sokalsky of the errors of Barrick's ways.

The meeting lasted for two hours. I could see from his occasional remarks that Sokalsky understood everything I have said. He did not argue with me. He said that what I was talking about was all very interesting and promised that he would read my paper carefully and give me a written answer. I have never heard from him since, nor have I heard from Randall Oliphant, the President of the company. Both men were fired later by Munk as shareholder dissatisfaction with the company's hedging policies, and with the low-altitude flight of the share price, could be heard inside of the bunker, sound-proofing notwithstanding. Scapegoats had to be thrown to the wolves to keep them away from the door.

I sold my shares and leaps, as did thousands of others. And I went back to my own den to lick my wounds.

If forward sales, why not forward purchases, too?

Barrick never explained to the world what has happened, or how they would fix the flawed policy. Even today, the new guy at the helm President Greg Wilkins defends the policy of 'a reasonable level of hedging' as an 'essential risk-management tool for the company'. It is supposed to 'stabilize revenues and satisfy banks that finance its projects'. But if this were true, then the policy should be made even-handed. Barrick has never admitted that its one-sided forward selling was responsible for the bearish bias in the gold market for the last decade of the century and the millennium.

In my paper I suggested an easy way to repair this bias. The company could complement its forward sales by forward purchases. These are triggered whenever the gold price is low and falling. Just as the gold mine lifts its short hedges as production is delivered into the hedge book, it can lift long hedges as deals to buy new gold properties are being closed out. In this way the mine can acquire new gold properties at the best possible price. I have evidence that Sokalsky understood my point perfectly well, the point being that the bias against the long side of the market would be removed as speculators would be coaxed back to it. Quite possibly my paper was in the hands of the top brass when they discussed the dismal failure of their policy of unilateral hedging, as it dawned on them with the new century and millennium. For all I know, Sokalsky could have proposed my idea of 'bilateral hedging' as a face-saving measure which, for him, could have been a 'skin-saving' measure as well.

Is Barrick a front to cover up gold-laundering?

That is, unless Barrick was a front to cover up gold laundering by governments, in which case unilateral forward selling was not a mistake but a deliberate policy. I couldn't help but believe that the company had a vested interest in suppressing the price of gold. Its ambition to become No. 1 also points that way. It is not about vanity. It is about pricing power. The suspicion that Barrick is a front to cover up a gigantic gold-laundering operation, presumably on behalf of a government (or governments) that need more time to complete a gold-acquisition program in the order of thousands of tons of gold, is hard to escape. Incidentally, if you interpret 'gold laundering' as a polite expression for 'stealing shareholder gold', no harm done.

Unfortunately, such a conspiracy theory will be very difficult to prove or disprove. I was not the only one who suggested it. GATA and Golden Sextant named Barrick as a co-conspirator in the illegal scheme to suppress the gold price.

When in the early 1990's Barrick sued the United States Treasury over a user-fee issue and, implausibly, won in the court, I failed to smell the rat. Only later did this lawsuit appear like a whale-size red herring to me, dropped to deflect suspicion away from Barrick lest someone think it was a front. "Behold, little David conquering the towering Goliath! What rubbish it is to suggest that David was bribed by Goliath to do it!" At about the same time Barrick moved its headquarters to shed its image as a maverick, to assume the image of a 'responsible corporate citizen'. No longer did it want to rub shoulders with hippies. Its credentials were established beyond the shadow of a doubt.

Achilles heel, or noose around the neck?

One analyst has called its hedge book Barrick's Achilles heel. But to others it looks more like a noose around the neck that no amount of 'creative book-keeping' or 'off balance-sheet financing' can hide forever. It has been stated publicly that Barrick would be bankrupt if it marked to market its liabilities. Wilkins gave himself till the end of 2009 to clean up the mess and reduce the hedge-book from 14.3 million ounces of gold to 9.5 million. But by that time the gold price could be well into four digits. The question is whether the kindly and gentlemanly bullion bankers will honor their 'no margin calls for fifteen years' pledge at those lofty prices. If shareholders can't throw the rascals out, maybe the bullion bankers can, and will.

Maximize life, not profits

In the meantime an even larger business challenge is confronting Barrick in the shape of a cost-of-production squeeze. Under a gold standard, the gold miner typically mines his property most conservatively. He goes after marginal grades of ore, the most expensive to exploit, where a base metal miner would go after the highest grades, the least expensive. The gold miner is not interested in maximizing profits as is the base metal miner. And for a very good reason, too. The marginal utility of a base metal declines. The miner wants to extract it from the bowels of the earth before the price may drop even more. By contrast, the marginal utility of gold is constant. There is no rush to dig it up only to bury it again in bank vaults. Therefore the gold miner wants to maximize the productive life of his mine, not profits. Barrick threw this wisdom of the trade to the winds as it has been mining the highest grades of ore available, and at break-neck speed to boot. Now it has to face the consequences. Its mined-out properties will have to be closed down prematurely, from which gold has been extracted and sold at what must, in retrospect, appear as give-away prices.

My suggestion of forward purchases of gold combined with the miner's problem of premature exhaustion of gold properties, would have made a perfect fit. Barrick would have been in an extremely strong position to buy new gold properties while lifting the long hedges it had put on when the gold price was much lower.

The Best Little Whorehouse in Nevada

Here is how a reporter described the scene at Barrick's annual meeting of the shareholders in Toronto's Metro Convention Centre last spring:

"The sky is dull grey, but the mood inside is dazzling. Pockets of spontaneous applause break out during the presentations. Standing at a podium emblazoned with the Barrick logo before a cinemascope-sized graphic display of the company's global reach, Wilkins leads shareholders through the past year's triumphs, and hints at a long and prosperous future for a company that now has unprecedented size and clout.

"He is followed by the 78-year old Munk, resplendent in a dark grey pinstripe suit, pale blue shirt and a luminescent pink tie. Munk pauses for effect and then leans over the podium. In a gravelly voice speckled with traces of his Budapest childhood, he delivers a rumination that is both self-congratulatory and self-deprecating, at once a nod to Barrick's humble origins and a prelude to a glorious future. 'I can't help but sit back and say that what we have done here has been spectacular', he says. 'But it's not the mines, it's not the reserves, [and] it's not the credit rating that's the best in the industry. What makes me proud, what makes me exceptionally happy, are the intangibles...those intangible values of integrity from which every decision automatically springs. It's the culture that this company has had in its DNA from the time it bought Camflo Mines'.

"You should give as good as you get. Integrity, as Munk says, means many things in gold mining, including paying people fairly for their work and contributing to local communities. It can even mean, he says puckishly, funding and building housing projects for miners in places like Elko, 'that dusty, miserable Nevada town with one whorehouse'."

Hey, Munk, wait a minute! It's all very well to fund and build posh whorehouses where miners and top brass can Barrick to their heart's content! But what about the share price? What about the patrimony of the shareholders?

Shareholders? They will be Barricked. Again.

I know it. I have been there.

Yours, etc.
Antal E. Fekete
former Barrick shareholder

References

Charles Davis, *So Big It's Brutal, Report on Business*,

The Globe and Mail: Toronto, June 2006, p 64-73
Bob Landis, Readings from *The Book of Barrick: A Goldbug Ponders the Unthinkable*, May 21, 2002

Richard Rohmer, *Golden Phoenix: The Biography of Peter Munk*, Key Porter Books, 1999

A.E. Fekete, *The Texas Hedges of Barrick*, May 2002

Ferdinand Lips, *Gold Wars: Will hedging kill the goose laying the golden egg?* pp. 161-167, New York: FAME, 2002

DISCLAIMER AND CONFLICTS

DERIVED FROM INFORMATION AND SOURCES BELIEVED TO BE RELIABLE, BUT THE AUTHOR MAKES NO REPRESENTATION THAT IT IS COMPLETE OR ERROR-FREE, AND IT SHOULD NOT BE RELIED UPON AS SUCH. IT IS TO BE TAKEN AS THE AUTHOR'S OPINION AS SHAPED BY HIS EXPERIENCE, RATHER THAN A STATEMENT OF FACTS. THE AUTHOR MAY HAVE INVESTMENT POSITIONS, LONG OR SHORT, IN ANY SECURITIES MENTIONED, WHICH MAY BE CHANGED AT ANY TIME FOR ANY REASON.

Posted Sunday, 13 August 2006

Professor Fekete's story lays to rest any questions about the purpose and efficacy of Barrick's forward-selling. Along with the Central Bank gold loaned to investment houses and sold, the forward-selling by Barrick and AngloGold Ashanti were together responsible for the collapse of gold prices in the 1980s and 1990s.

The war on gold has come at a steep cost to those who waged it. The Central Banks have not yet admitted how much of their gold is gone and will never be returned and the millions of ounces of gold forward-sold by Barrick and AngloGold Ashanti will cost their shareholders billions of dollars in losses.

The real losers, however, are the citizens whose gold was sold by their Central Banks to maintain a global monetary Ponzi scheme that created mountains of debt—debt that is now about to overwhelm everyone in an avalanche we call the *TIME OF THE VULTURE.*

2012 UPDATE: For years, Barrick suppressed the price of gold by selling forward (hedging) millions of ounces of gold at below market prices. Barrick had hedged 9.6 million ounces for delivery between 2011 and 2019 at $396 per ounce. But in September 2009 with gold already at $1,000 per ounce, Barrick was forced to take a loss of $5.7 billion and close its hedge book.

SECTION VII

INVESTING IN THE TIME OF THE VULTURE
IF YOU FOLLOW THE CROWD
YOU WILL FOLLOW THEM
RIGHT OFF THE CLIFF

Topic 31

...the stock market is a rigged game... It really is just a giant carny game, one in which there are only predator and prey, and precious few big winners. Wall Street's best and brightest may have more teeth and fewer tattoos than carny men, but they employ essentially the same skills in separating the gullible from their hard-earned dollars. Both try to convince us that "Everybody goes home a winner!" even though we know better. We always imagine ourselves winning the big stuffed panda, even though we know we'll be lucky to take home a pack of Marlboros or a Luke Skywalker keychain.

- RickAckerman, <u>www.rickackerman.com</u>

Rick Ackerman's comments are a direct result of his 12 years' experience as a market maker and industry insider on the floor of the Pacific Coast Exchange. Ackerman is also the author of Ric's Picks, **www.rickackerman.com**, an options newsletter predicting market turns, a strategy surprising in its accuracy. It is, however, Mr. Ackerman's cynicism about the investment industry that commands our attention here.

The investment industry is above all an industry. As in any knowledge-based industry, it purports to know more than others (which it does), and proceeds to leverage this knowledge for its own gain. The mistake is in believing that the investment industry, much like government, has your well-being as its primary goal.

The recommendations of industry analysts regarding Barrick Gold are a case in point. Silver and mining expert Theodore Butler points out in the following post the obvious disparity between Barrick's growing billion-dollar losses and the still-positive views of industry analysts:

Posted on January 3, 2006
http://www.investmentrarities.com/01-03-06.html

The almost $3 billion open gold loss on Barrick's books is greater than their cumulative total profits for the entire existence of the company. To my knowledge, it is the largest derivatives loss in history. I ask you to think about that for a moment. The world was atwitter with the recent $200 million copper loss by China, as well as the $500 million oil loss and bankruptcy by China Aviation Fuel (Singapore) last year. Barrick is set to report a $560 million gold hedge loss for the quarter, $1 billion for six months and almost $3 billion in total, and the financial world looks the other way.

According to Yahoo, of the 20 analysts covering Barrick, 18 rate it as a hold, buy or strong buy and 2 as a sell (there were no strong sale ratings). This, for a company that is holding the largest open trading loss in history. Why is that?

Butler's question regarding why 18 of 20 analysts recommend investors to hold, buy or strongly recommend a buy on Barrick Gold is a rhetorical one. The answer is obvious—investment analysts have always been more touts than analysts. Their role in the industry is to sell investments, not to protect the public from disaster.

Right up until the collapse of the dot.com bubble, investment analysts were still cheerleading tech stocks. So, too, it was with Enron. Three weeks after the Wall Street Journal reported Enron had hidden losses, 10 out of 15 Wall Street analysts still listed Enron as a "buy".

CAN WE TRULY EXPECT THOSE WHO AIM TO EXPLOIT US TO BE TRUSTED TO EDUCATE US?
- Eric Schaub

Because investment analysts by and large are industry shills, who are you to trust? From whom are you to seek advice?

SEEK ADVICE FROM THOSE
WHO UNDERSTAND THE PROBLEM
NOT FROM THOSE WHO PROFIT BY ITS CONTINUANCE

All of us are recipients of an unintended gift caused by the manipulation of the gold markets by the Central Banks and the collusion of government and financial interests. Their manipulation and collusion has created a strong and vibrant community of shareholders, investors, and analysts—a community that can now be easily accessed on the web, a community of experts whose thoughts and musings provide more than enough direction for those seeking advice in the time of the vulture.

The community itself is far larger than those who believe gold will be the only ark in the coming economic deluge. Its common thread is the belief that economic fraud cannot be sustained forever, that no matter how powerful the participants or how wealthy those who benefit, a house built on sand cannot and will not last forever.

A storm is gathering and those who hope the optimism of financial experts and industry touts will be justified are going to be more than disappointed in the days ahead—they will be bankrupted and broken by the events that are now about to unfold.

OPTIMISM OF THE OSTRICHES
FEAST OF THE VULTURES
FILL YOUR PLATES NOW
THE OPPORTUNITY
WON'T LAST LONG

Topic 32

I think we should put on another 100 points in the S&P 500 by next February and another 1000 points on the Dow.
- Peter Canelo, Canelo & Associates, 10/31/2006

Our feeling is that the economy is slowing and this is good news for investors.
- Abby Cohen, Goldman Sachs, 10/17/2006

The upside still outweighs the downside in our view...People forget—this isn't like the late 1990s. This is like the mid-1990s.
- Tony Dwyer, FTN Midwest Securities, 10/18/2006

I don't think the economy's 'landing.' I think the economy's doing great...It's better than Goldilocks quite honesty. This is the greatest global boom of all time.
- Ed Yardeni, Oak Investments, 10/18/2006

Count me somewhere between bullish and very bullish. The U. S. stock market remains undervalued, in my opinion.
- Bill Miller, Legg Mason, 10/21/2006

It simply is not remarked upon enough how unbelievably powerful, how unbelievably bullish this rally is.
- James Cramer, CNBC's "Mad Money," 10/27/2006

The fact is we can't find enough to worry about, and that's usually a good time to find value in the stock market...Any red ink between how and the end of the year is an opportunity and not something for investors to run from.
- Mike Williams, Toqueville Asset Management, 10/31/2006

...I think bravado and optimism begets bad times and chronic cautiousness paints a beautiful picture for the future. {This} is a low-risk, high-return situation created by cautious players.
- James Paulsen, Wells Capital Management, 10/20/2006

Could we have a big bear market? I don't think so. Bear markets come from a combination of positive sentiment with bad surprises virtually no one anticipates...Today too many gloomsters and not that many big-time boomsters (like me) are around for this combination to occur.
- Kenneth L. Fisher, Fisher Investments, 10/30/2006

These comments were excerpted from an article by Kevin Duffy of Bearing Asset Management. The article was posted on November 2, 2006 on **www.financialsense.com**, a website on gold and the markets. The purpose of Mr. Duffy's article was to showcase statements of investor optimism even as the economy teeters on the edge of disaster.

As absurd as these optimistic comments will someday appear, they are nonetheless important markers in the *TIME OF THE VULTURE*. While investors are still optimistic, there is still time to profitably invest in gold.

GOLD
AN ECONOMIC INSURANCE POLICY
FOR A COLLAPSING ECONOMY
THE *TIME OF THE VULTURE*
AND THE FIVE STAGES OF GOLD

- STAGE 1: THE SUPPRESSION OF THE PRICE OF GOLD Central Banks collude with investment banks and gold mining companies to force down the price of gold.

- STAGE 2: THE PRICE OF GOLD MOVES UPWARD. Gold begins to rise, doubling in price even as Central Banks fight its rise.

- STAGE 3: THE PRICE OF GOLD BECOMES INCREASINGLY VOLATILE. The price of gold is subject to increasing highs and lows as large investment funds move in and out of gold as global economic uncertainties wax and wane, a sign that gold is increasingly a haven in uncertain times.

- STAGE 4: EXPLOSIVE ASCENT IN THE PRICE OF GOLD. A crisis results in a monetary breakdown which drives the price of gold to never-before-seen highs. Investment capital floods towards the safety of gold. Central Banks capitulate.

- STAGE 5: THE PRICE OF GOLD STABILIZES. The crisis recedes and order begins to return to the markets. Though losses are substantial, a new order based on new realities slowly begins to emerge.

In 2009 we entered Stage 3 where, initially, few invest in gold because it is human nature to wait for the crowd before acting. In this case, waiting for the crowd insures only that this time you will be left behind—with the crowd.

LEMMINGS NEVER LACK FOR COMPANY
BENEATH THE NEED TO GO WITH THE CROWD
IS THE FEAR OF BEING ALONE

The days ahead will be among the most difficult. We have grown used to believing the future will be better than today. In the near future, however, and for some time, it will not be so and you had best be prepared.

2012 UPDATE: Today, the investors' desire for profit has been supplanted by the need for safety, a need that is increasingly problematic. Even US Treasuries, once considered the safest of paper assets are no longer considered to be the haven they once were.

On July 9, 2012 the *Financial Times* reported: *This year, investors have been gobbling up US treasuries in a desperate effort to search for safety…But during the financial crisis of 2007 and 2008, it became clear western dominance was crumbling, and the focus moved from the G7 to the G20…But now the G20 is looking impotent too; thus the world is trapped in a scary limbo. China and the other emerging powers are wary of taking a leadership role, but the west is declining. The net result then, is that nobody is in charge; it is an unstable "G-zero" world…*

…some financial players are now trying to adapt… some asset managers are now adjusting to an era of grinding instability… for the American government trying to sell treasuries, investor "adaptation" may come as a nasty shock.

This is a sea-change in investor outlook. Paper assets, e.g. stocks and bonds, no longer offer the potential for profit and/or safety they once did. In 2012, the sovereign debt, i.e. bonds, of all countries is suspect. In the *Time of the Vulture*, only gold offers safety and profit.

In 2007, gold was in stage two. Today, gold is well into stage three, the last stage where gold can be purchased before rising beyond the reach of most investors. Be forewarned. Be prepared. Buy now.

READY OR NOT
HERE IT COMES

Topic 33

Sometimes reality has a way of sneaking up and biting us in the ass. And when the dam bursts, all you can do is swim. The world of pretend is a cage, not a cocoon. We can only lie to ourselves for so long. We are tired, we are scared, denying it doesn't change the truth. Sooner or later we have to put aside our denial and face the world. Head on, guns

blazing. De Nile. It's not just a river in Egypt, it's a freakin' ocean. So how do you keep from drowning in it?
  - Meredith Grey, a fictional character played by actress Ellen Pompeo on the TV series Grey's Anatomy

On November 16, 2006, Dr. Milton Friedman, the leading intellectual apologist for paper money and professor at the University of Chicago, passed away. On the following day, also at the University of Chicago, Dr. Antal Fekete, an expert on monetary theory and proponent of the gold standard, spoke as an invited guest before an executive MBA class.

Dr. Fekete's talk was politely received but the MBA students were not to be easily swayed from the promises paper money offered. Due to the recent death of Dr. Friedman, Dr. Fekete spoke extemporaneously instead of delivering a prepared speech highly critical of Friedman's theories (Dr. Fekete's original speech is included in the addenda of this paper).

Nonetheless, Dr. Fekete cautioned the students about a world economy where money is disconnected from anything real, where $1.25 quadrillion of paper is deposited and cleared annually in a global economy whose aggregate value totals but $40 trillion—a ratio that begs the modern equivalent of the medieval question, how many angels can dance on the head of a needle.

In introducing Dr. Fekete, one of the MBA students presented a chart by Richard Russell, author of the long-running Dow Theory Letter. The chart showed a historical convergence between the Dow Jones Industrial Average and the price of one ounce of gold.

With gold then at 647 and the Dow at 13,120, Richard Russell's chart predicted that the Dow would plunge downwards and gold will explode upwards with the two converging between 13,000 and 600. Today, in March 2009, the Dow has fallen to 6,547 and gold has risen to 918. Both have made considerable progress to fulfilling Richard Russell's prediction of eventual convergence.

The students' resistance to Dr. Fekete's cautious words was understandable; optimism is what students seek as they make their way in an uncertain world. But even as Dr. Fekete spoke and the students listened, there was far more reason for caution than optimism.

On Monday November 27, 2006, the UBS/Gallup Index of Investor Optimism was at its highest level since January, having gained 43 % in just the previous three months. But on that same day, when investor optimism was at its peak, the Dow Jones dropped 158 points. Three days before, the US dollar had unexpectedly plunged and the markets were spooked.

On that same day, November 27th, Herb Greenberg of MarketWatch reported that George Muzea had turned bearish in mid-November. Muzea, who tracks insider selling for hedge fund managers, had observed that insider selling was surging along with investor optimism, a combination that predicted to Muzea a market downturn.

> *If you want to lose money over a long period of time, buy when insiders are selling and the public is bullish.*
> - George Muzea, Muzea Insider Consulting Services

In November, corporate insiders sold $8.3 billion of their shares while purchasing only $133 million, the widest margin since 1987 (a year when the stock markets cratered). Sellers included Microsoft's Bill Gates (tech), Google's Eric Schmidt (tech), and Kohl's Corp.'s William Kellogg (retail). The ratio of insider stock sales to purchases was 68:1.

Because of the high ratio of insider sales, Muzea told Greenberg to expect a "sharp and steep decline not unlike the one that hit the market last spring -- and maybe worse".

There were other signs of approaching economic problems as well. On November 1st, Fortune Magazine had reported that Liz Ann Sonders, the chief investment strategist at Charles Schwab & Co., had a chart so frightening she was hesitant to show it to investors.

Ms. Sonder's chart measured the National Association of Home Builder's Market Index (a monthly measure of builder confidence) against the Standard & Poor's 500 stock market index, with a one-year lag.

Jon Birger, a writer for Fortune Magazine, noted that Ms. Sonder's chart, over a ten year period, had predicted stock market advances and retreats with uncanny precision.

Not only did the NAHB index presage the start of the post-1994 bull market in stocks, but its decline starting in 1999 foreshadowed the equity market collapse that came the following year. Builder confidence rebounded in November 2001 - a year ahead of the stock market upswing that began in October 2002.

Birger wrote:

Why is Sonders worried now? Just look at the chart. **Over the past year, the NAHB housing index plummeted 54 percent. Were stocks to follow suit, the S&P - 1400 in late October - would be trading below 700 this time next year.** [note: On March 9, 2009, the S&P is trading at 677. It is my belief that the US Plunge Protection Team's market manipulation delayed and distorted the collapse of the S&P until recently; and, while the day of reckoning can be delayed, it cannot be prevented.]

The prediction of a 50 % drop in the S&P 500 answered one of the questions an MBA student had posed to Dr. Fekete.

IF THE MARKETS ARE OUT OF BALANCE
WON'T THEY SELF-CORRECT?

The answer is yes:

THE MARKETS WILL SELF-CORRECT
IN THE COMING ECONOMIC COLLAPSE

DR. MILTON FRIEDMAN'S FAITH IN THE MARKETS AND ITS SELF-CORRECTING MECHANISMS WILL SOON BE JUSTIFIED—ALBEIT POSTHUMOUSLY, BOTH FOR HIMSELF AND THE MARKETS.

"I don't think the macro statistics reflect accurately what's going on in many local markets," says Bruce Karatz, CEO of national home-builder KB Home. In many once-hot regions, order cancellation rates are running above 40 percent, new-home sales volume has dropped 50 percent, and new-home prices are down 10 percent to 25 percent. Karatz says the current downturn is worse than any he has seen - even the early 1990s market that left so many big builders reeling.
- Jon Birger, Fortune Magazine, November 1, 2006

Americans, of course, weren't aware of how bad conditions really were. This information wasn't seen on TV or on the front pages of America's newspapers, at least not then. Editors knew full well such stories conflict with crowd control, the hidden agenda that determines what Americans know and think about.

LOOK, ILLEGAL ALIENS ARE COMING ACROSS THE BORDER

Illegal immigration, gay marriage, and the death of Anna Nicole Smith are preferable to the corporate interests that keep America in a somnambulant coma as they go about seeking that one last pocket of hidden profits before the roof caves in.

The pockets of Americans, however, have already been picked and most available cash is long gone. What remains are credits cards, many of which are now over their limits, charging interest rates of 32 % and accruing exorbitant late fees.

No, it's not illegal immigration and gay marriage that is threatening America's way of life. Its credit and debt, the banks that issue them, the lobbyists and politicians that assist them and those that profit by its continuance.

MY ADVICE, AMERICA LAY OFF
JOSE, MARIA, AND THEIR KIDS
(AND TED AND MARK AND SUE AND MARY)
THEY ALREADY HAVE ENOUGH TROUBLE WITHOUT
BEING BLAMED FOR YOURS BECAUSE IT'S YOU WHO
HAVE BEEN ASLEEP AND ALLOWED YOUR FUTURE AND
THE FUTURE OF YOUR CHILDREN AND YOUR NATION

TO BE HIGHJACKED
AND WHILE IT'S TOO LATE TO PREVENT
WHAT'S ABOUT TO HAPPEN
IT IS NOT TOO LATE TO PREVENT
FURTHER DAMAGE IN THE FUTURE

The 2005 pay of the heads of America's top five financial services companies (Bear Stearns, Goldman Sachs, Lehman Brothers, Merrill Lynch, and Morgan Stanley) totaled $186,600,000, their average pay $37,320,000. Henry Paulson, head of Goldman Sachs, is now US Secretary of the Treasury.

John Mack, Morgan Stanley's CEO, currently under suspicion for allegations of insider trading received a 2006 bonus of $40 million; and Lloyd Blankfein, Chairman and CEO of Goldman Sachs, eligible for a 2006 $87 million bonus, received $53.4 million, giving Mr. Blankfein $91.4 million in compensation for 2005/2006.

PROXIMITY TO THE SPIGOTS OF CREDIT
DETERMINES WHO WILL PROFIT AND WHO WILL LOSE

Most of the MBA students who listened to Dr. Fekete aspired to become CEOs in these same investment banking and financial services companies and, of course, to be compensated accordingly.

But instead, the students were to encounter the self-correcting mechanism of "free-markets" in a particularly unpleasant way—for the majority of today's students and, indeed, most Americans, are now loaded down with unsustainable levels of debt.

As the 3rd edition of this book is being written, those MBA students who dismissed Dr. Fekete's words of warning are now most out on the street looking for employment. Many of the investment banks where they expected to work have collapsed.

IN THE COMING DAYS
PERSONAL BANKRUPTCY WILL BE
THE PRICE THAT MANY WILL PAY

DEBT
THE MILLSTONE OF AMERICA
CAN AMERICA EVER RECOVER

Topic 34

No country is free when it can't pay its debts.

This is the $65.9 trillion question that no one has yet answered. The July/August 2006 report from the St. Louis Federal Reserve Bank states that the future liabilities of the US are now so large they can never be repaid.

Bill Gross of the PIMCO bond fund has stated "the way a reserve currency nation gets out from under the burden of excessive liabilities is to inflate, devalue, and tax".

But when an insurmountable amount of debt exists, hyperinflation has traditionally been the exit-strategy of choice. And, unfortunately, under its current leadership America has been particularly bereft of viable exit-strategies.

WHAT IS TO BECOME OF AMERICA?

In America, the term fiscal conservative used to have real meaning. The term fiscal conservative, at the very least, described a Republican, one who shunned fiscal excess and promoted balanced budgets. It does no longer.

And, now, we as a nation have moved past the tipping point, the point at which known solutions will still work.

WHAT ARE WE TO DO?

The question is rhetorical, for while our collective response will affect our collective future, it cannot and will not save us from what is about to happen.

WHAT CAN I DO?

This is the question you must answer for yourself and your family. If you are in a position to reallocate financial assets, this analysis of current economic realities will be of value. At the very least, it will make clear what is about to occur and why it happened. But whatever your financial position, all your resources – financial, emotional, and spiritual - will be strained to their utmost in the days ahead.

FIND OTHERS
FIND SUPPORT
FIND DIRECTION

You must find others who understand what is about to happen. Share this information with friends and family. In the addenda, websites will be listed where you will find helpful information and advice. Do not face this crisis alone.

AVOID OSTRICHES

We are in the midst of a revolutionary paradigm shift. The resistance to change will be considerable. Choose your counsel accordingly.

THE TIME OF THE VULTURE
AND THE SWEET SPOT

The sweet spot in the Time of the Vulture will perhaps be the shares of junior gold mining companies. For information on the subject, see *The Perfect Option* by Jim Puplava and *The Perfect Option Part II*, at **www.financialsense.com**.

The shares of junior gold mining companies will outperform the large cap gold mining companies. To invest in this area, however, you must have competent and expert advice as it is highly volatile and subject to extreme risk.

For those seeking even greater returns, the warrants of junior gold mining companies offer twice the upside for those willing to take on additional risk. Warrants of junior gold mining companies are the bulls-eye center of gold's sweet spot. For more information, see **www.preciousmetalswarrants.com**.

The same caveat regarding risk also applies here.

Of particular interest, in the addenda that follows, Thomas Tan's article, *My View of HUI and Gold*, analyzes the price of gold versus the shares of large cap, juniors, and unhedged gold producers—Mr. Tan's thoughts about the future price of gold are especially interesting.

SILVER AND THE *TIME OF THE VULTURE*

Silver investments in *THE TIME OF THE VULTURE* may also prove to be very lucrative. Franklin Sander's article, *Why Silver Will Outperform Gold by 400 % and How You Can Join The Party* is well worth the read. The article is posted at **http://news.silverseek.com.**

2012 UPDATE: The manipulation of the price of gold extends to the shares of both senior and junior gold mining companies. This development has changed my initial enthusiasm for investing in junior gold miners.

Junior explorers with significant deposits will still sell for high multiples as senior mining companies will be hard pressed to replace their depleted inventories with new supplies. But the sweet spot in junior miners will be hard to find given the current price suppression of the gold sector.

Regarding the ongoing debate as to whether gold or silver will outperform, there are silver bugs and there are gold bugs. I am firmly in the gold camp but my bias is based solely on my appreciation for the metal itself, nothing else.

Silver may outperform gold—or it may not. Take your pick or pick both.

THE OLD PARADIGM COLLAPSES
A NEW PARADIGM EMERGES
THE BIRTH OF A NEW AGE

Topic 35

The more universal a paradigm, the longer its existence, the more fundamental and revolutionary will be its shift. The mother of all paradigm shifts is now underway.

Its essence: the rebalancing of universal polarities - yin and yang, the masculine and feminine. This revolutionary shift is being experienced as the rise of women in the world, the shift of power between the East and the West, and the current inability of male hierarchical power structures to solve critical social, political, and environmental problems.

We are living during a period of great change. The collapse of our global monetary system is but one indication that a significant and fundamental shift is in progress. Another sign of the shift in global polarities is the rebalancing of power between the East and West.

James Wolfenson, recent chairman of the World Bank, stated that within 25 years, the combined economies of China and India will exceed those of the Group of Seven, currently the world's wealthiest nations—the United States, Canada, Germany, the United Kingdom, France, Italy, and Japan.

Wolfenson pointed out that the rise of China and India will return the two nations to parity with western powers, a parity which had existed from the 1500s to the 1700s. The balance between East and West is being restored.

The return to parity between the East and West is part and parcel of a greater paradigm shift now underway—a shift that is rebalancing fundamental polarities on a global scale, a shift that is affecting not only global economic and political alliances but gender as well.

David Hackett Fisher's *The Great Wave* (Oxford University Press), a book of particular interest to economic historians, traces historical periods of economic stability and ensuing periods of inflation and instability. Fisher writes that we are in such a period today, a period of increasing inflation and instability that will culminate in a new social order.

Because the new paradigm is rebalancing the role and power of women, the resistance to the shift of power is especially obvious in areas and institutions where women have been repressed and subjugated. The rise of religious fundamentalism, especially in the US and Middle East, is a direct reaction to the rising power of women and the current shift away from a male-dominant paradigm.

Perhaps no one saw the advent of the new paradigm as clearly as Buckminster Fuller. Like his peers, the humanist Catholic philosopher Teilhard de Chardin and the brilliant Indian mystic, Sri Aurobindo, Buckminster Fuller was not constrained by the paradigm in which he was born nor the limitations of what others thought possible.

BUCKY WAS A FUTURIST
AND WHAT A GRAND FUTURE HE FORESAW

Buckminster Fuller's vision of the future was one of abundance and sharing, a vision quite at odds with that offered by today's corporations and political elites. Another of Bucky's contemporaries, Dr. Carl Jung, the famous psychologist, had a story regarding these conflicting visions.

The water of life, wishing to make itself known on the face of the earth, bubbled up in an artesian well and flowed without effort or limit. People came to drink of the magic water and were nourished by it, since it was so clean and pure and invigorating.

But humankind was not content to leave things in this Edenic state. Gradually they began to fence the well, charge admission, claim ownership of the property around it, make elaborate laws as to who could come to the well, put locks on the gates. Soon the well was the property of the powerful and the elite.

The water was angry and offended; it stopped flowing and began to bubble up in another place. The people who owned the property around the first well were so engrossed in their power systems and ownership that they did not notice that the water had vanished. They continued selling the nonexistent water, and few people noticed that the true power was gone.

But some dis-satisfied people searched with great courage and found the new artesian well. Soon that well was under the control of the property owners, and the same fate overtook it. The spring took itself to yet another place—and this has been going on throughout recorded history

- Excerpted from *Owning Your Own Shadow* by Robert A. Johnson
Published by HarperSanFrancisco, 1993 pp.vii-viii

Dr. Jung's story is especially relevant in these times. Those closest to the spigots of credit are unaware their water is about to vanish; and, while this may be bad for them, it could be good for the rest of us.

AMERICA 2.0

Topic 36

America, America
My country 'tis of thee
How did this come to pass
How did this come to be

In 1997, American historians William Strauss and Neil Howe published *The Fourth Turning*. Based on past historical cycles, Strauss and Howe predicted that another important turn in American history was now about to occur.

The next Fourth Turning is due to begin shortly after the new millennium. Around the year 2005, a sudden spark will catalyze a crisis mood. Remnants of the old social order will disintegrate. Political and economic trust will implode. Real hardship will beset the land, with severe distress that could involve questions of class, race, nation, and empire. Yet this time of trouble will bring seeds of social rebirth.

164

Americans will share a regret about recent mistakes—and a resolute new consensus about what to do.

The very survival of the nation will feel at stake. Sometime before the year 2025, America will pass through a great gate in history, commensurate with the American Revolution, Civil War, and twin emergencies of the Great Depression and World War II.

The risk of catastrophe will be very high. The nation could erupt into insurrection or civil violence, crack up geographically, or succumb to authoritarian rule. If there is a war, it is likely to be one of maximum risk and efforts—in other words, a total war.

- *The Fourth Turning,* William Strauss and Neil Howe,
Broadway Books, 1997

According to Strauss and Howe, the previous three "turnings" in American history were (1) the American Revolution, (2) the Civil War, and (3) the Great Depression in conjunction with World War II. The next, The Fourth Turning predicted by Strauss and Howe, is now underway.

In 2006 it cannot be said America is yet in a crisis mood. Perhaps that will come in 2007 or 2008, when mounting home foreclosures, an economic recession, and sinking stock prices will begin to take their toll [note: The crisis arrived in fall 2008 after the stock markets collapsed]. For America, however, the world is already forever changed.

The goodwill built by America after WWII is now gone. After 9/11, the rest of the world watched as America and England with only nominal support from others invaded Iraq in a bizarre and bilateral attempt to redraw geopolitical boundaries in the Middle East.

In pursuit of this ill-fated and ill-conceived war, America has publicly justified torture, kidnapping, government spying on its citizens, and the suspension of previously guaranteed liberties such as *habeas corpus.* And, as a result, America's moral authority to lead, like its gold, is now gone.

...the Constitution doesn't say that every individual in the United States or every citizen has or is assured the right of habeas corpus. It doesn't say that. It simply says that the right of habeas corpus shall not be suspended.

- Alberto Gonzales, US Attorney General

AMERICA VERSION 1.0 IS AT THE END OF ITS CYCLE
AMERICA VERSION 2.0 HAS NOT YET BEEN RELEASED

Empires, like products, come with expiration dates. Some products, like George Lucas' Star Wars and Tolkien's Lord of the Rings produce successful sequels; most do not. Empires, as a rule, fall into the latter category.

It is perhaps to America's fortune that its most recent attempt at empire was unsuccessful. Because America's immense influence in the 20th Century was built less on coercion than on the momentum of universal ideas such as freedom and opportunity, America has a chance to regain that which it so recently lost.

LEADERSHIP, UNLIKE POWER, IS BESTOWED
BY OTHERS ON THOSE BELIEVED DESERVING

Four markers, three obvious and one not, will be telling indicators if America can regain the moral authority to lead. The markers are:

GLOBAL WARMING

HONEST VOTING IN AMERICA

ISRAEL AND MIDDLE EAST POLICY

THE REPAYMENT OF BILLIONS OF DOLLARS
MISSING FROM THE AMERICAN INDIAN TRUST FUND

SECTION VIII

THE FIRST MARKER
GLOBAL WARMING

Topic 37

Today, perhaps no other issue is as important as global warming; and, perhaps no better example of America Version 1.0 exists. America's refusal to deal with global warming is tied directly to that which fuels the current version of America 1.0—corporate greed and power.

Only two nations in the world, the United States and Australia, have refused to ratify the Kyoto Protocol, the world's first collective effort to deal with the global warming. In 1997, by a unanimous 95-0 vote, the US Senate voted to prohibit the US from participating in the Kyoto Protocol's attempt to cap dangerous greenhouse emissions.

Of late, Australia, America's only ally in allowing market forces to destroy the planet, is having second thoughts. Australia is experiencing its worst drought in over 1,000 years, a drought that is sending farmers into bankruptcy in ever-increasing numbers and causing a rise in rural suicide rates.

It is doubtful, however, that Australia's dire plight will change America's mind about global warming. In fact, it is highly doubtful most Americans will ever know of Australia's extreme drought. The rest of the world has no idea how isolated Americans are from reality; and, perhaps more unfortunately, neither do Americans.

Previously an art, crowd control has been refined in America into a science; CNN in America does not resemble CNN in the rest of the world. China's government censors could learn a thing or two from America's ability to control what Americans know and think about. The difference between China's People's Daily and America's Fox News is essentially one of subtlety.

The selling of the Iraq war to Americans was accomplished with the support of a complicit media that silenced critics and promoted the war. Jeff Cohen, at MSNBC during the run-up to the invasion of Iraq, described the process in his article, *Inside TV News: We Were Silenced by the Drums of War* (**www.truthout.org**), excerpted from his book, *Cable News Confidential: My Misadventures in Corporate Media.*

The problem for US media was that there was wide disagreement among WMD [weapons of mass destruction] experts, with many skeptical about an Iraqi threat. The problem only worsened when UN inspectors returned and could not confirm any of the US claims...How did MSNBC and other networks solve the problem? Management favored experts who backed the Bush view - and hired several of them as paid analysts…As the war began, CNN news president Eason Jordan admitted that his network's military analysts were government-approved.

The fate of MSNBC's Phil Donahue Show is especially telling as Donahue, virtually alone in the US media, publicly opposed the invasion of Iraq.

As war neared, MSNBC Suits [management] turned the screws even tighter on "Donahue." They decreed that if we booked one guest who was anti-war on Iraq, we needed two who were pro-war. If we booked two guests on the left, we needed three on the right. At one staff meeting, a producer proposed booking Michael Moore and was told she'd need three right-wingers for political balance….. Three weeks before the invasion, MSNBC Suits terminated "Donahue," their most-watched program.

AN AMERICAN SUCCESS STORY
THE PRECISION BOMBING OF AMERICANS BY THE MEDIA

The US government convinced Americans to invade Iraq with the complicity and help of the US media—and they have done the same in successfully dismissing the dangers of global warming.

UNTIL AMERICANS HAVE ACCESS TO NEWS NOT CONTROLLED BY CORPORATE MEDIA, THERE IS LITTLE HOPE THAT AMERICA WILL REGAIN ITS ROLE OF LEADERSHIP IN TODAY'S WORLD

2012 UPDATE: The crowd control of Americans continues as the US energy cartel still prevents any slowdown of US carbon emissions; and although this year, 2012, is the hottest year on record and this month, July, over 2,000 US heat records have been broken, Americans are still in denial about global warming.

The tragedy continues.

THE SECOND MARKER
HONEST VOTING IN AMERICA

Topic 38

I don't see why we need to stand by and watch a country go communist due to the irresponsibility of its own people. The issues are much too important for the Chilean voters to be left to decide for themselves
- Henry Kissinger, former US National
Security Advisor and Secretary of State

Chile's democratically-elected government was overthrown by the CIA in 1973 and replaced by a US supported dictator. And Chile is not the only country in which the US decided the issues were too important to be left to the democratic process.

In 1953, Iran asked the Anglo-Iranian Oil Company (now British Petroleum) for an audit of the royalties due Iran. The British refused and instead asked for US help in overthrowing those who made the request.

The CIA did so, staging a coup [code named Operation Ajax], and successfully ousted Iran's popular democratically-elected Prime Minister and replaced him with a dictator more friendly to US and British oil interests, the Shah of Iran (see Wikipedia at **http://en.wikipedia.org/wiki/Operation_Ajax**).

FIXING DEMOCRACY IN AMERICA
Fixing: to make certain an outcome by illegal means

Unfortunately, the CIA disdain for the democratic process is no longer reserved for foreign countries. Former Director of the CIA and current Secretary of Defense, Robert Gates, was a key participant in replacing America's ballot boxes with electronic voting machines—machines that cannot be audited and leave no paper trail, necessary in determining if voter fraud has been committed.

The emergence of this fact about the subversion of democracy by electronic voting machines is due primarily to the efforts of a housewife and everyday citizen from Renton, Washington: Bev Harris, the founder of Black Box Voting.org (see **www.blackboxvoting.org**).

Ms. Harris has almost single-handedly uncovered the roots of the ongoing scandal behind electronic voting in America, a story recently chronicled in the documentary movie, Hacking Democracy, and featured on HBO just prior to the 2006 elections.

IF YOU CONTROL THE VOTE COUNT
WHAT'S NOT TO LOVE ABOUT DEMOCRACY?

In an Open Letter to the American People, published by the Baltimore Chronicle, Ms. Harris exposed the role played by members of the National Security Agency and CIA in the recent installation of electronic voting machines in America. And, for exposing what she has discovered, Ms. Harris and others have found themselves the object of intense US government scrutiny.

See Bev Harris' *Open Letter to America* at her website:

Her book, *Black Box Voting, Ballot Tampering in the 21st Century*, is available for download for at her website.

Ms. Harris' *Open Letter to America* tells what she learned in uncovering the players behind America's darkest secret—the highjacking of democracy by a bipartisan coalition of Washington insiders.

HAVA, the "Help America Vote Act", the congressional bill supporting electronic voting, was co-sponsored by a Republican and a Democrat, the recently forced-to-resign **CRIMINALLY CONVICTED FORMER REPUBLICAN CONGRESSMAN** Bob Ney of Ohio, and **DEMOCRATIC CONGRESSMAN** Steny Hoyer of Maryland.

HAVA, co-sponsored by Bob Ney (R) and Steny Hoyer (D), became law through the lobbying efforts of a little known organization called "VoteHere". On the advisory board of VoteHere was former CIA DIRECTOR AND SECRETARY OF DEFENSE, ROBERT GATES.

While the obvious beneficiary of vote fixing has been the Republican Party, the response of the Democrats has been more than interesting; it's been downright suspicious. When the Democrats lost the 2000 election under questionable circumstances, protests came only from the black Democratic members of the House of Representatives. To register a formal protest, they needed one member of the Senate to stand with them. Not one Democratic senator would do so.

In the 2004 Presidential elections when again the vote was suspect, again one senator was needed. This time, one Senator did stand, but only one in a token gesture where the Democrats as a party quickly accepted the losing verdict and possibility of fraud with—even for Democrats—uncommon acquiescence.

WHERE THERE'S SMOKE THERE'S FIRE BUT THIS TIME IT SEEMS THE FIRE MARSHALS ARE IN ON THE INSURANCE SCAM

Those who voted for the Democratic presidential candidates in 2000 and 2004 watched helplessly as the Democratic Party would not either challenge or investigate the two elections that have changed forever the destiny and course of America.

DEMOCRATS OPPOSITION PARTY OR ENABLERS IN ON THE TAKE?

In a troubling development, in February 2007, Bev Harris alerted voters about a bill introduced by the Democrats to "reform" voting procedures. Known as the "Holt Bill", introduced by Congressman Rush Holt (D) of New Jersey; the Holt bill *ALLEGEDLY DESIGNED TO PREVENT VOTER FRAUD INSTEAD DOES THE VERY OPPOSITE.*

THE CIA KEEPS COMING UP WHERE AMERICA'S ELECTRONIC VOTING MACHINES ARE CONCERNED

Bev Harris points out that only two companies offer the voting technology mandated by the Holt bill; and that the head of the advisory board of one of the companies (Populex) is none-other-than

Frank Carlucci, FORMER DEPUTY DIRECTOR OF THE CIA, former chairman of the Carlyle group, and former Secretary of Defense Donald Rumsfeld's college roommate.

With former CIA Director Robert Gates on the advisory board of VoteHere (the lobbying group behind HAVA) and former CIA Deputy Director Frank Carlucci heading the advisory board of a company that supplies technology for voting machines, Americans might feel that the democratic process in America is indeed well guarded—or they might feel otherwise.

UNDER THE HOLT BILL
A POLITICIAN—THE PRESIDENT—WILL HAVE
TOTAL CONTROL OVER COUNTING AMERICA'S VOTES

Bev Harris points out that under the Holt bill, *neither citizens nor candidates will be granted access to any records in order to accurately audit the voting process.*

Instead of protecting American voters from fraud, the Holt "election-reform" bill instead delivers Americans directly into the hands of the US government, instituting a system whereby states cede all control to the central government in regards to voting.

In regards to the proposed Holt bill, Alan Dechert, president of the Open Voting Consortium, states:

If passed, it [the Holt bill], *would BREAK the voting system in the states while establishing a dictatorship to handle things: the Election Assistance Commission ("EAC" or just "the Commission") with its four commissioners appointed by the president of the United States.*

FIXING THE VOTE ISN'T POLITICS
IT'S TREASON

If America 2.0 is to be in any way different from America version 1.0, Americans must be aware that those now in power—Republicans and Democrats alike—will use every means at their disposal to insure their continued power—even using the guise of reform.

ONLY ONE LOOPHOLE WILL BE NEEDED

The entire political system in America is broken. Power in both parties is concentrated at the very top where the National Committees of both Republicans and Democrats disburse the millions of dollars needed to run political campaigns. Such a tightly controlled top-down disbursement system virtually assures candidate compliance with donors' intent.

THE SAME CORPORATE INTEREST GROUPS
CONTROL AND CONTRIBUTE TO BOTH PARTIES
KEEP YOUR EYE ON VOTER REFORM IN AMERICA
IT WILL EITHER PERPETRATE PRESENT POWER SYSTEMS
OR IT WILL BRING TRANSPARENCY
AND NEEDED REFORM

> **2012 UPDATE:** Although the Holt bill never was signed into law, the manipulation of votes by easily compromised electronic voting machine continues. Until Americans demand fair elections, they won't get them.

THE THIRD MARKER
ISRAEL AND THE MIDDLE EAST

Topic 39

No one likes a crooked referee except the team being helped.

David Ben-Gurion, Israel's first prime minister, is often referred to as "the father of Israel." But in reality the patrimony of the Jewish state is more complicated. The actual patrimony of Israel should really be laid at the bedroom door of Winston Churchill. For without Churchill, the state of Israel would have remained as it had for over two millennia, a wandering people's distant dream.

History has been kind to Winston Churchill. It has remembered his many accomplishments and glossed over his many mistakes. But it would do us well to remember that the Palestinian-Jewish conflict of today is very much the deeply troubled child of its unacknowledged father.

It was at the behest of Churchill and England that after WWII the UN agreed to sponsor a Jewish presence in Palestine. When the King of Saudi Arabia was informed that "because of Nazi persecution" the Jews were to be given Arab land in the Middle East, the King reportedly replied: "Why don't they give them land in Bavaria?"

IN ORDER TO MAKE ROOM FOR THE JEWS
THE PALESTINIANS WERE MOVED OFF OF THEIR LAND
THIS IS THE CRUX OF THE ISRAELI-PALESTINE
CONFLICT

Winston Churchill's comment regarding this issue is remarkable for both his candor and callousness.

I do not agree that the dog in a manger has the final right to the manger even though he may have lain there for a very long time. I do not admit that right. I do not admit, for instance, that a great wrong has been done to the Red Indians of America or the black people of Australia. I do not admit that a wrong has been done to these people by the fact that a stronger race, a higher-grade race, a more worldly-wise race, to put it that way, has come in and taken their place.

- Winston Churchill on the projected removal of the Palestinians from their homeland

Racism is no more attractive coming from the mouth of a statesman than it is from the roar of a mob. The suppression of the rights of the Palestinian people has been ongoing since the end of WWII. It is no wonder that there is no peace in the Middle East; and, there will be none until this issue is resolved.

Ever the heir to England's fading dreams of empire, the US, after Churchill's death, took up Israel's cause, hoping that in Israel the US had a reliable pawn in its geopolitical aims in the Middle East.

THE JEWS HAVE MANY ATTRIBUTES
BEING A PAWN IS NOT ONE OF THEM

175

Though it may appear that the US-Israeli relationship has been without problems, it is not so. The US imprisonment of the Jewish spy, Jonathan Pollard has long been a thorn in the side of Jewish-American relationships; Israel wanting Pollard's release, the US refusing to grant it.

Even so, the US bias in favor of Israel has been overwhelming. Because Israel is perceived to be of strategic importance to US geopolitical interests in the Middle East, billions of dollars in US aid have been given to Israel and a blindeye has been turned to the most egregious of Israeli transgressions—both against the Palestinians and the US.

It is conservatively estimated the US has given $108 billion in direct aid to Israel, a rather stupendous sum; but what Americans don't know is what Israel has done to the US in return.

THE STORY OF THE USS LIBERTY

If Americans knew about the Israeli attack on the USS Liberty and the response by US government officials, there would be an instantaneous outpouring of sympathy for the US servicemen killed and wounded, rage at US officials then and now who continue to protect the perpetrators instead of those attacked; and there would be more understanding for the plight of the Palestinian people.

But the truth about what happened to the USS Liberty has been suppressed because the US government does not believe that it is in the interests of the US that Americans know about the brutal attack on the US surveillance ship—an attack that US government officials have since that day deliberately misreported in order to not offend Israel.

WHEN THE US GOVERNMENT
PROTECTS A FOREIGN STATE
INSTEAD OF ITS OWN CITIZENS
IT'S TIME FOR AMERICANS TO SERIOUSLY
RECONSIDER WHO THEIR GOVERNMENT
REALLY SERVES

On June 8, 1967 the US intelligence-gathering ship, the USS Liberty, was in international waters off the Gaza strip. Suddenly, unmarked Israeli aircraft attacked the defenseless reconnaissance ship and the Liberty radioed for help. In response, two US aircraft carriers based in the Mediterranean launched fighter aircraft WHICH WERE IMMEDIATELY RECALLED BY THE WHITE HOUSE.

Rear Admiral Geis called the White House to confirm the order.

> [Secretary of Defense] McNamara came on the line, then President Johnson. Johnson indicated to Geis that the aircraft were to be returned, that he would not have his allies embarrassed, and that he didn't care who was killed or what was done to the ship...the LIBERTY fell an easy victim to Israel's motor torpedo boat attack. FIVE torpedoes were lobbed at the Liberty, one hit amidships and instantly killed 25 sailors. A total of 34 died in the attack, 172 were injured.... The boats shot at American sailors on the deck of the Liberty as the sailors tried to help one another. As life rafts were put in the water by Liberty sailors in preparation for abandoning the ship, the boats shot them up. One boat pulled one out of the water and took it on board...The boats left the scene, apparently when they got erroneous word that the carriers had sent fighters to help the Liberty.

President Johnson later announced on TV that ten US sailors had been killed in an accidental attack. Orders were issued commanding that no one discuss the incident with anyone under penalty of court-martial. Excerpts that were posted at **http://home.cfl.rr.com/gidusko/liberty** further state:

> ....The attack has been a matter of controversy since 1967. Survivors and many key government officials including Secretary of State Dean Rusk and Joint Chiefs of Staff Chairman Admiral Moorer say the attack was no accident....Two Israeli officers have come forward to admit that the attack was no accident. Yet the Israeli government and its supporters insist it was a "tragic case of misidentification" and charge that survivors and their eyewitness supporters are lying.

Additional and on-going information about the USS Liberty is available at:
http://www.ussliberty.org/moorer3.htm and
http://www.ussliberty.org

THE RESPONSE OF THE US GOVERNMENT TO THE ATTACK
ON THE USS LIBERTY INDICATES THE EXTENT
OF THE POWER ISRAEL HAS OVER THE US

It should be noted that the current Israeli-Palestine conflict was not entirely unforeseen, especially by the person most responsible, Winston Churchill. The chief Middle East correspondent for The Independent, Robert Fisk, quoted from an essay Churchill had written in 1937 (**http://www.democracynow.org/2006/12/20/i_dont_think_we _westerners_care**) in an interview by Amy Goodman on the TV show, Democracy Now.

In the essay, Churchill ruminates on what his yet-unborn offspring, the state of Israel, might someday become and the problems it could encounter:

> *The wealthy, crowded, progressive Jewish state lies in the plains and on the sea coast of Palestine. Around it, in the hills and the uplands, stretching far and wide into the illimitable deserts, the warlike Arabs of Syria, of Transjordania, of Arabia, backed by the armed forces of Iraq, offer the ceaseless menace of war. To maintain itself, the Jewish state will have to be armed to the teeth and must bring in every able-bodied man to strengthen its army. But how long will this process be allowed to continue by the great Arab populations in Iraq and Palestine? Can it be expected that the Arabs would stand by impassively and watch the building up, with Jewish world capital and resources, of a Jewish army equipped with the most deadly weapons of war until it was strong enough not to be afraid of them? And if ever the Jewish army reached that point, who can be sure that, cramped within their narrow limits, they would not plunge out into the new undeveloped lands that lay around them?*
>
> - Winston Churchill 1937

With uncanny prescience, Churchill foresaw the future of today.

Israel, with US help, is armed to its teeth and the Arabs are no longer standing by impassively watching. The Saudis are now voicing an interest in developing nuclear capabilities, possibly as a counterweight to Iran's intended and Israel's present unacknowledged possession of nuclear arms; and, just as Churchill predicted, the Israelis have spilled over their borders intent on annexing more Arab land.

Mutual enmity fueled by religious differences and fundamentalist fanaticism on all sides is a heady mixture, a possible atomic powder keg waiting to be ignited and needing to be defused. The US invasion of Iraq has destabilized the Middle East and set in motion irreconcilable forces with the potential to engulf the region in mass conflagration.

On its way to fulfilling the dreams of its founding fathers, the US has been sidetracked by the lingering ambitions of England and the man who presided over its dying empire, Winston Churchill.

AMERICA NEEDS TO ATTEND FIRST
TO ITS OWN IDEALS AND DESTINY
INSTEAD OF THE DANGEROUS DREAMS
AND AMBITIONS OF OTHERS

2012 UPDATE: The US continues to follow the path of England, the declining imperial power of the 19th and 20th centuries; and, just like England, the US, too, is losing its grip on world hegemony. Tragically, US foreign policy still mimics England's wars of aggression in the Middle East and Afghanistan and supports Israel's national interests over its own.

Beginning in 2013 the US has promised to give $3.1 billion per year in military aid to Israel while cutting programs and benefits for its own citizens.

THE FOURTH MARKER
THE REPAYMENT OF BILLIONS OF
DOLLARS MISSING FROM THE AMERICAN
INDIAN TRUST FUND

Topic 40

Most Americans have never heard about the billions of dollars missing from the US Government Indian Trust Fund. Indeed, Americans are still not even aware that the gold in Fort Knox has been gone for more than a half a century.

The following article posted at
http://www.yesmagazine.com
might shed some light on this long-denied scandal about the billions owed to America's Indians.

Fall 2005 Issue: ***Respecting Elders, Becoming Elders Indicator: Native American Trust Fund Reform Urged***

by Patricia Powers

A nine-year court battle by Blackfeet accountant and banker Elouise Cobell has prompted a coalition of American Indian leaders to propose a multi-billion dollar settlement to Indians and dramatic reform of the Indian trust fund. The proposal may be implemented in federal legislation being introduced this year. The trust fund has been unable to account for billions of dollars in oil, gas, and land-use royalties the government has collected on behalf of an estimated 500,000 individual Indians. Indian leaders estimate the amount owed to be at least $100 billion.

For decades, Cobell has sought to change policies and practices of the U.S. Department of Interior that deny Indian families land-use profits owed them. In 1996, she filed a class action case (Cobell v. Norton) on behalf of 300,000 Indian families. A federal judge hearing the case in 1999 said the accounts were so botched that it was impossible to know what was owed to whom, especially since Interior had destroyed hundreds of boxes of documents. Officials of several U.S. administrations have been held in contempt of court for failing to account for the monies, and the federal courts were placed in charge of overseeing the process of fixing the trust funds.

The Allotment Act of 1887, intended to assimilate Indians into American society, divided 90 million acres of reservation land into individual lots called allotments. The federal government awarded allotments to tribal members, but took charge of these lands and leased them to gas, oil, timber, grazing, and mining companies. About $300 million a year flows into the trust fund. That money was supposed to be passed to the Indians, but Interior's Bureau of Indian Affairs often failed to do so. Despite complaints and congressional investigations, Native Americans have never received all the money due.

Both the Clinton and Bush administrations refused to settle the case, but in June [2005], tribal leaders converged on Washington to urge a $27.5 billion settlement and offer a set of 50 principles for reform of the trust fund. Senators John McCain of Arizona and Byron Dorgan of North Dakota are sponsoring legislation to implement many of these recommendations, including fixing the trust system without taking money away from other Indian programs, reallocating splintered lands, and assuring proper future accounting of Indian trust funds. After 118 years and with compound interest owed, according to federal courts, the price tag is enormous. Indian leaders regard the $27.5 billion figure as significantly discounted.

Many American Indian communities are desperately poor and tribal governments are chronically short of funds to pay for health care and education.

— Patricia Powers

For more information, go to **www.fcnl.org**. Patricia Powers is a member of the Friends Committee on National Legislation, Native American Advocacy Program.

Reprinted for "Respecting Elders, Becoming Elders,"
the Fall 2005 YES! Magazine, PO Box 10818, Bainbridge
Island, WA 98110, Subscriptions: 800/937-4451
Website: **www.yesmagazine.org**

HONOR IS MEASURED NOT BY WHAT IS DONE TO THE POWERFUL
BUT BY WHAT IS DONE TO THE POWERLESS

If America's Indians were white, Republicans, and members of America's ruling elite, an offer to settle for pennies on the dollar would not be on the table. Instead the full amount plus interest and damages would be the topic of discussion and $200 billion and counting would be the starting point for settlement—and, of course, there would on-going criminal and civil charges for conspiracy and embezzlement brought to bear.

THE $200 BILLION QUESTION
WHO GOT THE MONEY?

The answer is not difficult to discover—unless, of course, those in power don't want the truth known. Moneys were deposited. Checks were written. Moneys were paid. Tracking the money trail is not rocket science. It is well within the ability of law enforcement to discover who received the money and to then set the wheels of justice in motion—hey FBI, care to lend a helping hand on this one? Oh, I'm sorry, I forgot who you work for.

This is, however, America Version 1.0 and in America Version 1.0 law enforcement is reserved primarily for those who transgress against the established order, not its members who are close enough to loot its coffers and steal what belongs to others.

In America Version 1.0, the powerless and less fortunate are forced to beg for what is rightfully owed and due. In America Version 1.0, it is Halliburton and the well-connected friends of the military-industrial complex who take what they may, legally looting America's wealth; while those like the American Indians, who are rightfully owed billions, get nothing except a cold shoulder (with more than a little help from the courts, Congress, law enforcement, and the

Presidency)—and the continuing denial and ignorance of the American people.

IF GEORGE BUSH WERE AN INDIAN
HE WOULDN'T BE IN THE WHITE HOUSE
HE WOULD BE OUTSIDE IN THE OUTHOUSE

Dealing from a stacked deck is illegal in Las Vegas, but it's legal in Washington DC where politicians, legislators, and judges are bought and sold behind closed doors.

There, everyone has his or her price and it is willingly paid because the payback is more than worthwhile and the money paid isn't theirs in the first place; and that, my fellow Americans, is just how it's done in America Version 1.0—at least for now.

TO BE RELEASED
AMERICA VERSION 2.0
WHAT IT WILL LOOK LIKE
IS COMPLETELY UP TO YOU

The uncertain always look to the certain for leadership. Unfortunately, that alone is usually sufficient.

2012 UPDATE: On December 8, 2010, the US government settled Indian claims against the Indian Trust Fund for the sum of $3.4 billion. The original sum was $40 billion but when the US Court of Appeals refused to order the US government to give an accounting of the missing funds, it was clear that Indians would be forced to be satisfied with pennies on the dollar. In 2010, that happened.

As of July 2012, no moneys have been distributed. The national disgrace continues.

Section VIII

ADDENDA LIST

ADDENDUM I

DARRYL ROBERT SCHOON'S GOLD LIST OF INVESTMENT ADVISORS

These are perilous times. Expert counsel and direction is needed to traverse what is to come. The investment advisors listed below are the best I have found. It is yours to decide which one (or two or three etc.) best fits your situation. Remember: Today, the highest risk is to be found in following yesterday's advice. The times have changed. Plan accordingly.

Read the websites carefully and pick the advisors you prefer. Then discuss your choices with trusted friends and family. You can change your strategy at any time. We live in a world of change and a portfolio should shift when conditions shift. A good advisor will counsel accordingly.

www.zkb.com (services not offered to US citizens)

www.goldcore.com

www.goldmoney.com

www.bullionvault.com

www.perthmint.com.au

http://sprott.com/products/sprott-gold-precious-minerals-fund/

http://www.bmginc.ca/

www.kitco.com

www.dowtheoryletters.com

www.simplyprofits.org

www.financialsense.com

http://kingworldnews.com

www.rickackerman.com

www.adenforecast.com

www.agorafinancial.com

www.dinesletter.com

www.hsletter.com

www.the-moneychanger.com

http://www.amazon.com/Paper-Money-History-Evolution-Currency/dp/0964306611 (This book by author and coin dealer, Ralph T. Foster [email: tfdf@pacbell.net], will convince readers why owning gold and silver is so important.).

ADDENDUM II

AN INTERVIEW WITH JOHN EXTER
BY FRANKLIN SANDERS

John Exter was unique among Central Bankers in his understanding of money and the markets.

Simplex munditiis -- elegant simplicity -- was the rule the Roman poet Horace laid down for the uttermost refinement of taste. Nor does aesthetics disagree with economics or other sciences, for science always prefers the simplest theory which explains the greatest number of facts.

Alas, our fickle human minds grow forgetful. Over the years simple, timeless truths lose the glitter of novelty or become so universally accepted that we forget how brilliantly they shone when new. Watts' steam engine no longer interests us for its novelty, although in its day it revolutionised the western world. Although the microchip is changing our world today, after 20 years' exposure it is a commonplace.

Today the monetary truths which Mr. John Exter enunciated for 40 years -- the gold standard, the danger of debt, a deflationary economic collapse -- have become (in some small circles, at least) unchallenged axioms, but when he first began to explain them he was practically alone. Now that the evidences of a deflationary depression are undeniable, it is fitting & profitable to return to this hard money pioneer & re-examine our foundations.

John Exter is one of the world's most knowledgeable individuals on international banking & the US Federal Reserve System. Over the years he has known the world's most important central bankers on a first name basis. His experience has given him a unique foundation for understanding the monetary events of the past 80 years.

Born in 1910, Mr. Exter went to graduate school determined to discover what had caused the devastating Great Depression. After graduating from the College of Wooster (1928-1932) he went to the Fletcher School of Law & Diplomacy &, in 1939, to Harvard for graduate work in economics.

After a stint at MIT during World War II, Mr. Exter went to the Board of Governors of the Federal Reserve System as an economist. In 1948 he served first as adviser to the Secretary of Finance of the Philippines, & then to the Minister of Finance of Ceylon (now Sri Lanka) on the establishment of central banks. He became the first governor of the newly organised Central Bank of Ceylon in 1950.

In 1953 Mr. Exter was named division chief for the Middle East with the International Bank for Reconstruction & Development (World Bank). In 1954 the Federal Reserve Bank of New York appointed him vice president in charge of international banking & gold & silver operations.

Mr. Exter left the New York Fed in 1959 to join First National City Bank (then the world's second largest bank, now called Citibank) as vice president. In 1960 he became senior vice president. As an international monetary adviser for the bank's International Banking Group he had special responsibilities for relations with foreign central banks & governments. In 1972 he took early retirement to become a private consultant.

Mr. Exter is a member of the Council on Foreign Relations (CFR), the Committee for Monetary Research & Education, the Mont Pelerin Society, & other groups & boards too numerous to recount. He & his wife Marion have four children. He very kindly made time for this interview on June 14, 1991.

MONEYCHANGE - After your remarkable consistency over the years, it now seems your predictions are coming to pass. Before we concentrate on that, let's talk a little bit about your background. I was intrigued to learn that you had gone to graduate school with Paul Samuelson, America's most unrepentant Keynesian economist.

EXTER - [*laughing*] I'll say I did, yes. I knew him at Harvard graduate school.

MONEYCHANGER - You arrived at Harvard about the same time that Keynesianism got there?

EXTER - Keynes published his famous book, *The General Theory of Employment, Interest, & Money*, in 1936. I went to Harvard graduate school in the fall of 1939, 3 years later. By that time the principal professors of economics at Harvard had just grabbed Keynesianism

& run away with it. It was like a new religion.

The leading Keynesian at Harvard was Alvin Hansen. His sidekick was John Williams. Williams was much more circumspect, much more doubtful about Keynesianism. When I later became a vice president of the Federal Reserve Bank of New York in charge of foreign operations, Prof. John Williams' office was next to mine. He wasn't only a professor of economics at Harvard specialising in money & banking, but also a vice president of the Federal Reserve of New York for years & years. That may have been the reason I got the job: I got along much better with him than with Alvin Hansen.

I should not say that I rejected Keynesianism right away. I had it pumped into me in those early years & actually taught it in the entry level economics course at Harvard. As the years wore on I became more & more sceptical. In 1943 I went to the Radiation Laboratory at MIT & ultimately became the assistant to the director of the laboratory. I helped Paul Samuelson get a job there, & from time to time we had lunch together. On one occasion Paul leaned over to me & said, "John, are you or are you not a Keynesian?"

I answered, "Paul, I have my doubts -- serious doubts." I was not yet ready to take him on.

Later I did take him on, after I became Senior VP of Citibank. We met from time to time through those years, attended the same conferences, & were always antagonists. I was always in the minority -- there were very few people on my side. Most were Keynesians, or, later on, Friedmanites.

MONEYCHANGER - At the bottom they don't differ much from each other.

EXTER - They differ some. Both believe in government intervention in the economy, although Friedman restricts his intervention to the Federal Reserve, which is the worst intervention of all. They fight, too, but not as strongly as I have fought both of them. I put it right out on the table. In 1962 I was in Boston to make a speech to the [*corporate*] Treasurers' Club of Boston for Citibank. I had the morning free, so I thought I'd call on Paul Samuelson. He was right across the river at MIT.

We immediately got into a terrific argument about why the dollar was weak & why we were losing gold. I had worked 10 years with the Federal Reserve system by that time, so I said, It's simple: the Fed is printing too many dollars & they flow out of the country into foreign central banks who demand gold.

When Samuelson denied all this I asked him, "Paul, what do *you* think is the reason the dollar is weak?" He replied that the increase in productivity in Europe & Japan was more rapid than in the US. Luckily Japan was in trouble at that time, so I said, "Why do you think Japan is worse off than we are?" I cannot remember his reply but I said, No, that's not it. "Well, what do you think?" he shot back.

I said, Paul, I don't think: I *know*. It's because the Bank of Japan is running its printing presses even faster than the rest of the central banks around the world are running theirs, even our Fed's. When he tried to argue against that I said, Paul, I *know* about this because the Bank of Japan has just been to Citibank for a loan. We sat around the table & talked about the reasons for it & required the Bank of Japan to tighten money. He was nonplussed. "Well, John," he said, "you could be right -- but you're *lonely*." [*laughing*]

As a matter of fact it was that very year, 1962, when I saw the same problem at the Federal Reserve. President Kennedy had pressured Federal Reserve Chairman William McChesney Martin to run the printing presses, to expand money, & Martin had given in. While I was VP of the Federal Reserve Bank of New York from 1954 - 1959, Martin was chairman of the Board, so I came to know him intimately. Later as a Citibanker in the '60s I called on him regularly in Washington.

I saw Martin knuckle under to Kennedy & begin to run the Fed printing presses. The Fed got locked into an expansionism it dared not stop & became a hopeless prisoner of its own expansionism. Reserve Bank credit was about F$25 billion in 1961. It is about F$290 billion today. [i.e., in 1991. *A 1,160 % increase. - - Ed.*]

I immediately began to buy gold, which was then F$35 an ounce. I understood that this monetary expansion would go on & on, so I have recommended gold ever since. In 1968 I went 100 % position into gold. Americans were prohibited from holding gold, but we could hold rare coins. The Treasury had declared sovereigns to be rare [*laughing*] even though they weren't really rare at all. I could buy sovereigns for F$9.00 each. [*Today they're about F$85 each. - Ed.*] A sovereign is a little less than a quarter of an ounce, so I was buying gold at about F$36 an ounce. I was also buying gold mining shares for income.

When Nixon closed the gold window on August 15, 1971 I was 60 years old. Normal retirement age was 65, but on my own initiative I could retire at 60. I realised at once that I should not spend another four years in the bank, so I become a private consultant in domestic & international money (which I still am). Since 1968 I had been recommending a 100 % gold position. That has proven absolutely fabulous advice for those few who took it.

MONEYCHANGER - In 1984 I compared 1964 & 1984 prices in terms of paper, silver, & gold. In terms of gold the 1984 prices were 20 to 30 % of what they had been in 1964. In relative purchasing power, gold has been a consistent winner over that time, in spite of the frustrating '80s.

Keynesians have mostly favoured a one-world currency -- one fiat currency to circulate around the world.

EXTER - Keynes to my memory never wrote about that, but the idea has always been widespread. Long after Fed Chairman William McChesney Martin retired, I heard him at a meeting advocate a one-world currency, so this has been in men's minds for many, many years. They're trying now to establish a single currency in Europe. I don't mind that so much, if Europe wants it, but this present world-wide fiat paper money -- what I call "IOU nothing" money -- is going to break down. We're headed for the worst economic catastrophe in all of history. Obviously the best one- world money would be gold, the good old gold standard, but that is a pipe dream now.

MONEYCHANGER - You make a point that is extremely important historically: since 8/15/1971 the *entire world* has been on an unbacked paper money system. That has never before happened in history.

EXTER - Yes, I say that over & over again. That's why we are heading into such a catastrophe: the whole world has gone off gold. Without central banks, such a catastrophe could not be possible. Single paper currencies without gold backing have collapsed, going way back to John Law in France, our own continental dollar, & the French Revolutionary *assignat*, all in the 18th century. In this century I myself remember three different German marks: the mark until after WW I, the *Reichsmark* until after WW II, & since then the *deutsche Mark*. Two German currencies have just become worthless in my lifetime.

MONEYCHANGER - The unbacked paper money system has proven itself so successful in its repeated national collapses that governments & central bankers want to try it on an international basis. That doesn't make a bit of sense.

EXTER - It's *impossible*.

MONEYCHANGER - You recognised very early that one major problem with Keynesianism was its reliance on debt.

EXTER - That's what my upside-down debt pyramid is all about. The debt burden at some point becomes unsustainable because too many debtors borrow short term & lend long term, or, worse yet, borrow short term & put the money into bricks & mortar. [*Exactly the crisis that erupted in Asia in 1997 – Ed.*]

MONEYCHANGER - Exactly. Because most people thinking about inflation back in the '70s were looking at the models of John Law or Revolutionary France or even Germany after WW I, they saw our inflation ending in a hyperinflation. You have steadily insisted that our inflation would end in a deflation & a debt collapse.

EXTER - Yes, that's very important. I'm sure the collapse that I'm talking about will start in the dollar. (My debt pyramids are always in single currencies: there's a dollar debt pyramid, a deutsche Mark debt pyramid, a Yen pyramid, & so on.)

This will be a deflationary collapse rather than an inflationary blow-off because creditors in the debt pyramid will move down the pyramid [*See pyramid chart -- Ed.*] out of the most illiquid debtors at the top of the pyramid -- junk bonds, failing banks, S&Ls & insurance companies, Donald Trump, & Campeau. [*Trump has survived until now, 1998, but Long Term Capital Management & other ailing hedge funds fit the same bill. -- Ed.*]

Creditors will try to get out of those weak debtors & go down the debt pyramid, to the very bottom: currency (dollar bills), even though they pay no interest. Next above currency are Treasury bills, issued by the government & backed by the Federal Reserve, which supports the market through its open market operations. They are by far the largest component of Reserve Bank credit, so are really as safe as currency notes, plus they pay interest. Still, you can't buy anything with Treasury bills; you have to liquidate the bills to get money of some sort to buy something. [*The very flight to quality that we are seeing in 1998. -- Ed.*]

The higher debtors sit in the pyramid, the less liquid they are. At the top are all the least liquid debtors that I've already mentioned. This explains why we are headed for deflation. Creditors will move out of debtors high in the debt pyramid as many of those debtors fail through defaults & bankruptcies. That is very deflationary.

Did you know the public has already begun to go for currency? In 1989 currency in circulation increased F$11 billion; in 1990, F$27 billion. We have already had a major run down the debt pyramid into currency in circulation. Creditors have also run into Treasury bills. That is why Treasury bill rates have fallen faster & further than commercial paper rates.

MONEYCHANGER - As manifested by 2-1/2 times as much cash being put into circulation without any particular effect on prices. [*Compare the Fed's announcement that it would put an extra F$150 billion in circulation to ease Y2K-induced cash hoarding. This extra cash demand adds more deflationary pressure. -- Ed.*]

EXTER - That's a very important point. This increase in currency in circulation has gone under the mattress. It was not needed to make purchases. You don't buy many things with cash other than groceries & gasoline. Instead we use credit cards or write checks. So this currency was not demanded for commerce but for safety.

That's a tremendous increase -- you can follow these figures in *Barron's* & the *Wall St. Journal.* A month or so ago currency year on year was up F$29 billion. Since the highest previous increase in the history of the Federal Reserve system was about F$13 billion, this is far more total currency in circulation than ever before. Much of it has certainly been bought to be put under the mattress.

MONEYCHANGER - It hasn't shown up in prices or in bank deposits.

EXTER - We got along with an increase of only F$11 billion in 1989. That's all we needed then to buy goods & services, so the bigger increases since then must certainly have been stashed away.

The final step down is out of the debt pyramid altogether into gold. Do you know that at F$360 an ounce, it would only take about F$18 billion to buy up a whole year's worth of newly-mined gold? This increase in currency in circulation would have done that with F$9 or 10 billion to spare. Of course, if the public had bought gold instead of currency, the price of gold would be several hundred dollars higher than F$360 an ounce.

MONEYCHANGER - Just as your debt pyramid sits on a *tiny* golden point that supports a huge superstructure, that door of escape called the gold market is *very narrow.* There is not much room for many people to squeeze through that door.

EXTER - Right. People do not realise how scarce gold is. There just isn't that much gold around! Nobody knows exactly how much, but there's only something over 100,000 tonnes, maybe as much as 110,000 or even 120,000. Annual production has been around 1,500 tonnes for many years. Right now it's a little more, 1,600 or 1,700, but that's a very small increase in the total gold stock, 1.7 % or so. [*A metric ton of gold is 1,000 kilograms or 32,150 troy ounces. 1997 gold mine production was 2,464 tonnes, but central bank lending, forward sales, option hedging, and implied disinvestment added another 773 tonnes to supply. This* *"phantom supply" could not be foreseen in 1991. - Ed.*]

MONEYCHANGER - Not enough to affect the price significantly.

You say that this increase in currency in circulation is a sign that creditors are moving down the debt pyramid. Another giant sign is the insolvency of the S&Ls --

EXTER - That's what they're getting out of, weak S&Ls, weak banks, weak insurance companies. They're getting out of all those illiquid debtors at the top of the debt pyramid & going down to currency at the bottom.

MONEYCHANGER - You understood years ago that the problem was the expansion of this debt pyramid. We're left wondering just how long it can keep on building. There are two limiting factors. The first is psychological: how far human will confidence stretch without breaking? The second is an accounting problem: how much debt burden can the economy stand before the interest bite chokes off all economic activity?

EXTER - That's right. I thought of this upside down debt pyramid when I was at Citibank in the early '60s. I first gave talks on it inside the bank, trying to influence the bank because I saw too much borrowing short term & lending long term. It was just awful! I kept on warning the bank, but was just brushed aside. When Nixon closed the gold window I said, "This is my chance to get out," so I took it. [*laughing*] It was a great move on my part because I could buy gold & gold mining shares when gold was F$50 an ounce or less. Now Citibank is on the problem list because it has so many bad assets.

MONEYCHANGER - What particular signs currently make you think we're getting close to the collapse of the debt pyramid?

EXTER - The most important one is this flight to currency. It is bigger than anything I expected right now. We are still having troubles with banks, thrifts, insurance companies, & others, which will cause *more* people to move down to Treasury bills & currency.

At some point they will go to gold. We're at the threshold of that point. When they go to gold instead of currency or Treasury bills, the price of gold will take off. It will be a bandwagon everyone will want to get on. Then even those who have bought currency will see how foolish they were & that gold is far better to hold than currency, that it is the best store of value money man has ever found. It's stupid for people to hold currency. The Fed can simply print all they want at very low cost. Paper money is as abundant as leaves on trees.

MONEYCHANGER - When that happens, however, it won't be simply a larger number of people investing in gold: overnight it will become a buying panic. All that backs those Federal Reserve notes is *confidence*. When that breaks, there's no safety net at all. The financial system will just fall 50 stories & hit the pavement.

EXTER - That's right, but most people unfortunately will not recognise this until they see the price of gold shooting up. Gold has been in the doldrums for a full decade, & many people have concluded it's a bad investment. Those who bought currency instead of gold just did not understand what they were doing. They knew they wanted to get out of deposits because they were afraid of the banks & S&Ls. The only sure refuge they knew was currency. It may be the "coin of the realm," but it's still only paper IOU-nothings.

MONEYCHANGER - The instinct is correct, but the means is wrong. The government & the Fed have intentionally kept Americans ignorant of the advantages of gold. After 40 years of planned ignorance it's no wonder so few understand gold's value. In effect they are running to gold, but it's *paper* "gold". It's the same intent & motive.

EXTER - They don't realise that gold is money, the best store of value money that man has ever found over thousands of years. Also, gold is money world-wide; dollars are money only in the United States. So it is not Americans only who have been stupid: it is people the world over.

MONEYCHANGER - When a number do realise it, we'll have the problem of *very many people* trying to press through a *very small door* all at once. That can only happen if gold's price rises very, very rapidly. You're looking for a world-wide depression. That would clear out the debt bubble that's built up over the years & liquidate the bad debt. How long will that last?

EXTER - The rest of my life & longer. It'll be decades. This will be an economic catastrophe on a scale never before seen in history. We can see it coming now. Even in the published figures, deposits are shrinking. Bank & thrift balance sheets are shrinking by much more than the figures published by the Federal Reserve, because many assets have not yet been written down & they are getting worse & worse by the day. We have had more than three decades of heady expansion. We have now entered a merciless contraction from which gold is by far the best escape.

I've been a banker. Obviously a bank is most reluctant to write down bad assets. It hurts the balance sheet too much. The authorities have forced banks & thrifts to write the bad assets down, but they have a long way to go. The figures that you read today are too high -- they're really lower, but no one knows how much lower. It is hard to sell bad assets. This has been Seidman's problem in the Resolution Trust Corporation & the FDIC. He takes over weak banks & thrifts, & then it takes him *so long* to liquidate. Whether it's commercial real estate or residential, it's very difficult in this kind of market to liquidate those assets.

MONEYCHANGER - Certainly not for anything like full value.

EXTER - And it's not going to get better.

MONEYCHANGER - Anyone buying those assets would be out of his mind to pay more than 30-50 % of their loan value.

EXTER - That's right, & taxpayers absorb the losses.

MONEYCHANGER - One question really puzzles me. In past conversations you have described yourself as a "product of the establishment." Your résumé certainly shows your experience in the financial establishment. You have been one of the people who actually run the financial machinery of this country. Why can't the others see what you have seen?

EXTER - Oh, boy, that is a good question.

MONEYCHANGER - Destroying the currency destroys their own interests. Whether you look at the Federal Reserve system as a monopoly or cartel, or as a government agency, still their interests should be the same: stability & enhancing the value of their paper currency, not destroying it. Why can't they see that? It's a mystery to me.

EXTER - It's a mystery to me -- maybe less of a mystery because I've been a loner for so many years. That's why I told you the Paul Samuelson story: "Well, John, you could be right, but you're *lonely*!" That story reveals a lot. Incidentally, Paul was quoted in the *Wall St. Journal* as saying that he never thought he would live to see runs on banks again. So there is a only a small group that understands. You are in that group, but you're a loner, too.

I've battled Friedman more than Samuelson, mainly because Samuelson has been a professor all his life. Friedman left the University of Chicago & went out to the Hoover Institute at Stanford. We're both members of the Mont Pelerin Society; he is a past president & one of the founders. Many in the Mont Pelerin Society are on my side, but a majority of the members are monetarists, *i.e.*, Friedmanites. Friedmanism dominates Mont Pelerin Society meetings. There are no Keynesians of whom I am aware.

In a book published in the late 1950s Friedman laid out his view. The key was that the Treasury should sell off all its gold in the marketplace over a period of 5 years, go to floating exchange rates, & have the Fed increase the money supply at a fixed rate every year -- he didn't give the rate. [*laughing*]

When I read that years ago it shook me to the core -- he went further than Keynes had gone. Keynes had said, "The gold standard is a barbarous relic. It makes no sense to dig gold out of the ground in South Africa & put it back into the ground at Fort Knox."

Everybody had heard that, but Friedman went two steps further than Keynes, so in many respects he's been *worse* all these years, even though he professes to be a free marketeer.

These two schools of economic thought, Keynesianism & Friedmanism, have been taught in colleges & universities for decades now. Paul Samuelson's textbook.

MONEYCHANGER - I used that textbook in school, & it's terrible.

EXTER - Yes, it is awful. Samuelson doesn't regard gold as money at all, doesn't even see it as the best store of value. Why am I such a loner? Because these two schools of thought swept the world -- not just this country, but the whole world -- & I had to be very independent-minded to resist.

MONEYCHANGER - Even today, when the bankruptcy of both Friedmanism & Keynesianism is undeniable, they still cling to it. Both have obviously worked against the best interests of the government, the Federal Reserve, & the nation, if you understand those interests to be financial stability.

EXTER - Absolutely. Take a man like Walter Wriston, former head of Citibank. He was enamoured of Friedman -- often had him speak to the officers. I had to sit helplessly & listen.

MONEYCHANGER - Turning my question upside down, does the government or the banking system have an interest that is served by this debt expansion?

EXTER - Yes. Citibank *grew*. From maybe a F$15 billion bank when I joined it in 1959 to a F$230 billion bank recently [*A 1,533 % increase. -- Ed.*]. Growth was especially rapid in the big oil boom. Citibank led the way in so-called "re-cycling": accepting short term petro-dollar deposits from the oil producers, especially those in the Middle East, & making what have turned out to be long term loans, especially in South America. I thought it was bad banking, but by then I was a helpless retiree.

MONEYCHANGER - So they do have an interest.

EXTER - Ohhh, a tremendous interest. Citibank at one time became the world's biggest bank. Now the 10 biggest are in Japan; the whole banking system just turned around. It was a catastrophe, an absolute catastrophe, but there was nothing I could do to prevent it. Immediately after Nixon closed the gold window I made talks inside & outside Citibank, explaining that this meant we had gone to floating exchange rates: no more stable exchange rates, no more fixed exchange rates.

You may remember the Smithsonian Conference at Christmastime, 1971, when the world's monetary authorities tried to perpetuate fixed exchange rates. Who was there? Arthur Burns, chairman of the Federal Reserve Board; Paul Volcker, Under-secretary of the Treasury; John Connally, Secretary of the Treasury. These & others of similar stature from countries all over the world met at Smithsonian thinking that they could re-establish fixed exchange rates without going back to the gold standard. It was preposterous. I called this a giant exercise in futility. They did fix rates, but they only lasted a little over a year.

In January, 1973 I happened to be in Zurich & called on the president of the Swiss central bank, Fritz Leutwiler. He said, John, I'm going to have to get out -- I'm going to stop buying dollars to hold the rate. He did it in late January '73. There were people like him who understood the stupidity of it all, but not in the United States.

MONEYCHANGER - That's so strange. In spite of our monetary sins in America, there has also been a strong contrary tradition of monetary probity. That the people who run the financial system & the banks would just go crazy is hard to believe.

EXTER - I have witnessed it. There were a few people very strongly on my side, like the Governor of the National Bank of Belgium, Maurice Frere, a great man. He was president of the Bank for International Settlements at the same time, so I knew him intimately. After we had both retired, he & I would go to IMF meetings & bemoan what was going on. He was much older than I, but more than anyone he helped me strengthen my own convictions. He understood what was happening, & was dead against it, just as I was. Another one was Karl Blessing, president of the German Bundesbank. Both were giants in the community of central bankers.

MONEYCHANGER - What do we do from here? Keep on buying gold?

EXTER - Yes. I still recommend being 100 % in gold, or almost so.

MONEYCHANGER - You would stay in gold & gold-mining stocks?

EXTER - I'm for 100 % in gold & gold-mining stocks to this day. When the gold price does start to take off, it will reach a point where it will simply jump. In 1982 gold jumped F$40 in one day. I expect to see bigger jumps.

MONEYCHANGER - Was that the Mexican crisis?

EXTER - Absolutely right.

MONEYCHANGER So there's not really much point in talking about an upside price target for gold, is there?

EXTER - No. There's no target. The price will go through the roof & I don't know what government reactions to that will be.

MONEYCHANGER - Thank you again for your time & your courtesy.

My conversations with Mr. Exter have given me a new perspective on the banking problem. Even though central banking & fractional reserve banking form a terrible system, as long as there were men with character, that system could be made to work. Those men understood that there were monetary laws as fixed as the law of gravity, & respected them. It was a bad system, but by substituting character for gold, it could be made to work -- for a while.

But those sober, reflective people in banking have disappeared, replaced by time & the grandstanding speculators an inflation always spawns. Fractionalised banking is the child (or is it the mother?) of politics, & sooner or later politics will demand its due. Frail human character, in the face of politics, is no substitute for gold.

Franklin Sanders, **Franklin@The-Moneychanger.com**

Addendum II

ADDENDUM III

AUTHORS NOTE:

If Dr. Antal Fekete had a parallel lifetime he would have made an excellent insurance investigator. Insurance companies would have at their disposal a mind that would intuitively sense when something was amiss and any fraudulent claims would be decisively dismissed.

But in this lifetime, Dr. Fekete has had a higher calling than giving actuarial tables a fighting chance in the game of life. We are fortunate that Dr. Fekete turned his considerable mind and talents towards something that concerns us all—the issues surrounding money and the markets and how it affects all of us.

If you have a real interest in these areas, I could do no better than to point you in Dr. Fekete's direction. The world has strayed a long distance from that which works for all, a system that rewards producers, distributors, consumers, and savers alike. If we are going to make our way back, or perhaps even forward, his counsel will be invaluable.

WHERE FRIEDMAN WENT WRONG
"Is a gold standard cum real bills an option"

by Antal E. Fekete
Professor Memorial University of Newfoundland
"Dismal Monetary Science"

I was in Chicago on November 17 to address the MBA class of 2007 at the University of Chicago Graduate School of Business. I had a prepared address on Milton Friedman's monetary theories concerning the adjustment mechanism of foreign trade under the floating exchange rate system. Before I could deliver it the announcement came that Friedman had died the previous day in San Francisco at the age of 94. Newspapers carried long obituaries calling him the man "who has changed economics, policy, and markets" and "made free markets popular again". My address was sharply critical of the Nobel laureate Chicago economist. It would have been a dissonant chord in the cacophony of eulogies, so I decided to deliver an extempore address instead. However, I did not tear up my script. A dollar crisis was brewing. As I see it, Friedman has sowed the wind and the world is going to reap the whirlwind. Soon. When it does, I may want to publish my critique of Friedman's monetary theories.

Here it is.

Keynes and Friedman

Mr. Humphries, Graduating Class, Honored Guests, Ladies and Gentlemen:

You may call me reckless for daring to come here, the shrine of monetarism, to preach the anti-monetarist gospel. I must confess that I do it with some diffidence, given the enormous prestige of the father of monetarism.

Along with John Maynard Keynes (1883-1947) Milton Friedman was the enfant terrible of twentieth-century economics. Thirty-five years apart, the two of them were the great wreckers of the gold standard. George Schultz, a friend of Friedman's who served in the Nixon administration, says that in 1968 Friedman wrote a letter to president-elect Nixon suggesting that upon inauguration he should unilaterally take the United States off the gold standard (or whatever was left of it after president F. D. Roosevelt had wrecked it, on advice from Keynes, 35 years earlier in 1933).

In 1933 Keynes set out to persuade Roosevelt to default on the domestic gold obligations of the United States. He prevailed. In 1968 Friedman set out to persuade Nixon to default on the international gold obligations of the United States. He did not prevail. Not immediately, anyway. Thus the glory for dealing the coup de grâce to the gold standard eluded him.

Demonetization of gold was not the only option available to Nixon. He could have also devalued the dollar in terms of gold. As is known, Mises was in favor of the latter. A new official gold price of $70 per oz, amounting to a 50 percent devaluation, was the figure being bandied about.

Friedman's unsolicited advice to Nixon tells us something about the character of the man. Rather than initiating a high-level debate among monetary economists on the disastrous monetary policies of the US government that has led to the 1968 crisis, Friedman preferred to work behind the scenes on his plan to plunge the nation headlong into irredeemable currency. He was determined to make the dollar an out-and-out fiat money, the worst type of currency known to man.

Friedman knew that people would be hooked on fiat money once it has been inflicted on them. Here is a quotation from monetary scientist Walter E. Spahr [1], the Head of Department of Economics at New York University from 1927 to 1956.

"The majority, when given a taste of it, embrace irredeemable currency. The arguments offered in its defense are many and various, and constitute a sad commentary on human intelligence and character. The dilemma whether to give it up is much like that of the drug addict whether to give up dope. Even if he wanted to heed the advice of his understanding and experienced physician, often he will decide not to kick the habit. The run-of-the-mill speeches and articles on 'inflation' in this country provide a typical example of the majority reaction: they either evade the issue in ignoring that inflation is caused by fiat money, or they distort pertinent evidence, or they preach virtue where there is none, or they utilize currently popular platitudes, or they treat superficiality as though it should be accepted as wisdom. Rarely does one see a statement that an irredeemable currency is preferable accompanied by an attempt to give reasons for such an untenable belief."

Friedman's is such a statement.

"A nation in due course pays severely for the use of irredeemable currency. The United States is in a position analogous to that of a drug addict administering a law liked by all other fellow drug addicts."

In this case the 'understanding' physician, Friedman, urges the addict to carry on with substance abuse.

Addendum III

Irredeemable currency is massive fraud

The following quotation is also from Walter E. Spahr [2].

"Irredeemable currency means either fiscal or moral bankruptcy, or both. We are morally bankrupt now in so far as our monetary system is concerned. Both the U.S. government and the Federal Reserve have demonstrated that they wish to be free of pressure that people may put on them if our currency were redeemable. They are satisfied to hide behind irredeemable I.O.U.'s. Although a private citizen can expect imprisonment if he issues irredeemable bills of credit, our government and Federal Reserve banks have adopted as defensible a standard of morality that is not tolerated among honest people. They exercise power arbitrarily while refusing to accept the corresponding responsibility."

Friedman has never addressed the question of morality in issuing obligations that one has neither the means nor the intention to meet — as demonstrated by the check-kiting scheme between the U.S. Treasury and the Federal Reserve.

"A nation is in serious trouble when that state of affairs exists. The federal spending orgy since 1933, the depreciation in the purchasing power of our dollar, the mounting federal debt, the centralization of power in Washington, D.C., the steady march into the Death Valley of socialism, these are some of the manifestations of what tends to happen when a government steals the people's purse, having drugged them with the poison of irredeemable bills of credit."

This was written in 1958. Much happened since that would have surpassed even the worst fears of the author had he lived to see it, including the dismantling of America's once flourishing industries.

"Irredeemable currency is a massive fraud on the people. It is the chief and common means by which governments put shackles on free men."

In spite of all his free-market rhetoric, this point was lost on Friedman.

"A government loses its moral standing among men of integrity when it employs irredeemable I.O.U.'s. The regime of irredeemable currency is a monument to the dishonor of governments."

And, one might add, to the dishonor of advisors urging the government to carry on this abuse of power, in defiance of the Constitution.

"Irredeemable currency tends to expand and grow, and to carry abusers to their destruction. It is a potent contributor to international economic disintegration."

To this day Friedman could not see the signs of disintegration, be it the accelerating increase of the money supply, or the Babeldom of foreign exchange derivatives trading at the rate of $ 500 trillion per annum, and rising exponentially, when the combined GNP's of all the nations on earth is a paltry $ 40 trillion per annum.

"Irredeemable currency is a cesspool in which economic disease and human conflict are spawned. It is a wrecker of people, of families, and of nations. It is a road to the despotism of dictatorship."

It was, in Russia in 1917; in Germany in 1933; in China in 1949, to mention but three outstanding examples. Does Friedman really believe that it cannot happen here?

In most cases irredeemable currency led to war or civil war. Does Friedman really believe that it won't this time?

"Irredeemable currency is a symptom of a great national sickness. It 'engages all the hidden forces of economic law on the side of destruction which not one man in a million is able to diagnose' (according to Keynes, writing in 1919)."

Apparently, nor is Friedman the one in a million.

"What is the meaning of a gold standard and a redeemable currency? It represents integrity. It insures the people's control over the government's use of the public purse. It is the best guarantee against the socialization of a nation. It enables a people to keep the government and banks in check. It prevents currency expansion from getting ever farther out of bounds until it becomes worthless. It tends to force standards of honesty on government and bank officials. It is the symbol of a free society and an honorable government. It is a necessary prerequisite to economic health. It is the first economic bulwark of free men."

It is a great tragedy of our age that Friedman, the self-styled defender of the freedom of the individual and the free market, could not see this. Nor could he see the wisdom of Thomas Jefferson's warning: "If the American people ever allow bankers to control the issuance of currency, first by inflation and then by deflation, corporations growing up around them will deprive people of all their prosperity until their children wake up homeless on the land that their fathers have gained for them.

Floating or sinking?

In the 1950's Friedman concocted his pseudo-theory purporting to show how the floating system of foreign exchange rates would provide an automatic adjustment mechanism to balance the external accounts of trading nations. By implication, a gold standard was not a prerequisite of bringing about equilibrium in foreign trade. To say that Friedman is not a friend of the gold standard is an understatement. He maintains that it is a "price-fixing scheme" and as such a gold standard is anathema to the free market.

A monetary scientist should know better. Friedman puts the cart before the horse. A gold standard does not fix the price of gold any more than the tail wags the dog. What happens is that, once gold is in circulation, it is the price of bonds and notes that governments and banks are all too anxious to stabilize in terms of the gold coin of the realm. If they can, gold gives their obligations unmatched respectability. If they can't, then well-informed people will make their own conclusion about the quality of their paper.

According to Friedman's theory, under freely floating foreign exchanges a country in deficit would experience a loss in the exchange value of its national currency vis-à-vis a country in surplus which would, in turn, experience a gain. The former would be a more attractive market to buy from and less attractive to sell in. It could now export more and import less. The latter would be a less attractive market to buy from and more attractive to sell in. It would now export less and import more. The resulting changes in the export-import cocktail would restore trade balance. This is supposed to work as an automatic adjustment mechanism balancing foreign trade through the system of variable exchange rates.

This is an inept rationalization of the misfortune to have abandoned sound money. To say, as Friedman does, that debasement of the currency is a legitimate means of eliminating trade deficits, when carried ad absurdum, is saying that the worst currency is the best and the best the worst. Friedman's theory was actually put to into practice by Nixon. The result judged from thirty-five years' of perspective was an unmitigated disaster. The monetary, financial, and economic stature of the United States is in shambles, thanks to Friedman's floating dollar. As a matter of fact, the euphemism 'floating' should be interpreted as 'sinking'. It was the sinking dollar that has turned the country from the greatest creditor into the greatest debtor the world ever knew. The dollar used to be a monetary giant, the envy of the rest of the world. Now, it is a dwarf treated with contempt abroad. And the worst is still to come. We are facing a credit collapse.

Floating did not solve problems that the United States was facing in 1968. It made them worse. The devaluation and the deliberate debasement of the dollar did not make American exporters stronger. It made them weaker. The weak dollar was a huge bonanza for the foreign competitors of America. They were able to buy more imported goods per unit of exports. By contrast, Americans were able to buy less. The deficit was financed by an unprecedented debt-pyramid spinning out of control. The terms of trade for America has deteriorated to such an extent that it necessitated the wholesale dismantling of once prosperous American industries. It is not just the foreign purchasing power of the dollar that is on skid row. So is its domestic purchasing power, official doctoring of statistics notwithstanding. The widely fluctuating value of U.S. Treasury bonds is a butt of some very unkind jokes by foreigners. True, the American people still appear to be well off. But this prosperity is resting on "thin ice" in the words of former Federal Reserve Board Chairman Paul A. Volcker.

What caused the Great Depression?

In their "Monetary History" published in 1963 Friedman and Anna Schwartz blamed the Great Depression of the 1930's on the 'Great Contraction' of the money supply in the United States during the period 1929 to 1933. This is where Friedman went wrong. He mixed up cause and effect. In reality the contraction of the money supply was the effect of the Great Depression, not its cause. Businessmen declined to borrow in spite of the extraordinarily low interest rate available, because they could not see any profitable business opportunities around. The Federal Reserve can print all the dollars bills it wants; what's the use if there are no takers? The idea of putting crisp Federal Reserve notes into circulation through helicopter-drop, attributed to Friedman by Bernanke, is puerile. There is no synthetic substitute for the enterprising spirit of businessmen in search of entrepreneurial profits. You can't push dollar bills down the throat of lethargic businessmen.

The real cause of the Great Depression eluded Friedman, as it did Keynes before him. It was found by the German economist Heinrich Rittershausen who in looking for it went farther back in history than any other economist.

Unnoticed by Friedman and Schwartz, 1909 was a milestone in the history of money. That year, in preparation for the coming war, France and Germany decided to concentrate monetary gold in government coffers. They stopped paying civil servants in gold coin. To make this legally possible the notes of the Bank of France and the Reichsbank were made legal tender. Most people did not even notice the subtle change. Gold coins stayed in circulation for another five years. It was not the disappearance of gold coins from circulation that heralded the destruction of the world's monetary system. It was the making of bank notes irredeemable, even if they circulated side-by-side with gold coins for the time being. There was an early warning sign: the fact that finance and treasury bills were 'crowding out' real bills from the portfolio of central banks in consequence of the French and German governments' decision to make bank notes legal tender. Thus did the clearing system of the international gold standard fall victim to sabotage. It took twenty years before the chickens of 1909 came home to roost.

Well, come home they did with a vengeance. However, by 1929 the memory of the 1909 sabotage faded. No one suspected that a causal connection existed between the two events: making the bank notes legal tender and the wholesale destruction of jobs twenty years later. Permit me to elaborate.

Real Bills Doctrine

Friedman calls himself a 'monetarist', meaning that he is a devotee of the Quantity Theory of Money. Like all quantity theorists, he is a sworn enemy of Adam Smith's Real Bills Doctrine. He has never understood completely the market in real bills as it existed before World War I, the function of which was to serve as the clearing system for the international gold standard.

When the victorious powers dictated their peace terms after the cessation of hostilities, they intentionally disallowed the international bill market to resume its former functions. They wanted foreign trade to follow a political rather than an economic agenda, in this case, to keep their former adversaries on short leash. At the same time, they wanted to retain the outward trappings of a gold standard. They failed to realize that sooner or later the gold standard would seize up without the support of its clearing system, the bill market. Worse still, they failed to see that world trade would contract severely as a consequence. Worst of all they were too obtuse to understand that the elimination of the bill market would be followed, albeit with some lag, by a horrendous and intractable unemployment problem confronting the entire world. This was correctly foreseen and predicted by Rittershausen in 1930. See [3] and [4].

Had the victors allowed the market in real bills to resume its proper functions after the signing of peace treaties, world trade would have recovered quickly and the international gold standard would have continued to hold sway over the world. On advice from upright economists sensible governments would have realized that legal tender laws were thoroughly bad and would have removed them from the books. The charters of central banks barring finance and treasury bills from the portfolio could not have been violated with impunity. In that milieu there would have been no great depression. World trade wouldn't have vanished. The horrendous word-wide unemployment would have never occurred.

Destruction of the wage fund

The fact of the matter is that prior to World War I wages of the majority of workers, namely all those engaged in the consumer goods sector, were financed by the international bill market. This is a point that eluded not only Milton Friedman but Ludwig von Mises as well. They missed the fact that the consumer was the ultimate paymaster and he would pay on the dot, provided that he had access to gold. It was his gold coin with which all wages were paid under the gold standard cum real bills. Tampering with the bill market, the clearing house of the gold standard, had an inevitable, if delayed, deleterious effect on employment.

Payment of wages is due long before the final sale of merchandise to the ultimate gold-paying consumer. In some cases the employer paying wages may have to wait as long as three months before he can collect his share of the proceeds from the sale of merchandise. Thus, then, there is the problem of financing wage payments. Unless this problem is solved satisfactorily, mass unemployment will ensue. The wage fund cannot be financed out of savings. Under the gold standard it was financed through the spontaneous circulation of real bills.

Whenever certain goods were in urgent demand, their movement through the channels of production and distribution was financed by self-liquidating credit. This also included all wages payable to workers handling consumer goods that were moving along on their way to the final consumer through the 'assembly line', as it were. The credit was liquidated out of the proceeds of the sale: the gold coin given up by the ultimate consumer when he removed the merchandise from the market. The system worked admirably well. Bills drawn on the retailer would circulate spontaneously. Real bills enjoyed ephemeral monetary privileges, which treasury bills and finance bills did not. Producers could buy supplies against this credit, and they could discount these bills at the bank to get gold coins with which to pay wages. Bills were the most liquid form of earning assets in existence. The competition of banks for them was keen.

It is no exaggeration to say that the discovery of the spontaneous circulation of self-liquidating credit is one of the great achievements of the human intellect, on a par with the discovery of indirect exchange. Without it the great economic progress in the Modern Age would be unthinkable.

After World War I the victorious powers, led by blind hatred for the vanquished, wanted to make foreign trade bilateral instead of multilateral. Exports and imports were made subject to political rather than economic considerations so that the victors could discriminate against their former adversaries. In this effort they unintentionally ruined the natural system of financing production and payment of wages. They dissipated the wage fund. They blocked the spontaneous circulation of self-liquidating credit in the world, the only safe and sound source from which wage payments could be financed. In doing so not only did they deal a mortal blow to the gold standard but, inadvertently; they brought upon the world the curse of massive and persistent unemployment.

This problem has been haunting the world ever since. There is still no satisfactory way of financing the wage fund of workers in the consumer goods sector in the absence of a gold standard cum real bills. There is no way bills could circulate under the regime of irredeemable currency. Not because real bills are anathema to Friedman; but because the idea of a real bill maturing into paper money is preposterous. A real bill is a future good. It must be maturing into a present good such as the gold coin in order to be able to circulate. It would just not circulate if it matured into another future good such as a bank note, redeemable or not.

The wage fund couldn't be financed out of savings. Apart from the problem that saving takes time, the sums involved are far too large. The idea that the working class can save the funds out of which it can pay wages to itself is no less preposterous than the idea that soldiers in the field can lift themselves up by their own bootstraps.

The only alternative to a gold standard cum real bills is the regime of irredeemable currency. But then the government has to assume the responsibility for paying the handouts of the welfare state: it has to pay workers for not working, and farmers for not farming. Tertium non datur: there is no third alternative. The regime of irredeemable currency and the so-called welfare state are Siamese twins. Here, in a nutshell, is Friedman on the horns of a dilemma. He likes irredeemable currency while he dislikes the welfare state. But if you like irredeemable currency, then you had better like its corollary, the welfare state as well. Nor does the problem end there, since fiat money cannot be a permanent arrangement of society. Unless it is stabilized by returning to a gold standard, it will collapse after having caused a lot of mischief in the economy, as convincingly demonstrated by monetary theory and history.

Optimal rate of increasing the stock of money

Of course, Friedman says he has a panacea in mind for all the economic ills of the world. Just entrust the issuance of high-powered money at a steady optimal rate to the Federal Reserve. He was jubilant when his mentor Arthur Burns was named as chairman of the Federal Reserve Board. If anybody, he could do it! He could put the tenets of monetarism into practice. Well, he didn't. Neither could other chairmen, Bernanke's 'apology' on Friedman's 90th birthday notwithstanding. Central bankers consider Friedman's prescriptions "impractical" and they have said so. Friedman retaliated by quipping that "even a clever horse can thrash out grain at a steady rate, so why can't the dummies at the Fed?" There is neither inflation nor deflation in the never-never land of Friedman.

The idea that there is an 'optimal rate' of increasing the stock of money, and it could be determined scientifically, is chimerical. Creditors would challenge the 'optimal rate' saying it is too high; debtors would fight it saying it is too low. The federal government, being the greatest debtor of them all, would apply pressure on the Fed in support of the latter.

If the power to increase the money supply is delegated to an agency dressed in scientific garb, then this agency is a front behind which impostors hell-bent to usurp unlimited power under false pretenses hide. No matter how you look at it, the power to issue the currency is unlimited power. Unlimited power means unlimited corruption.

Mene Tekel Upharsin

In so far as Friedman has any coherent theory of money at all, it is the tenet that, even though the creation of wealth must be trusted to private hands and to the free play of the market, the creation of money must not — notwithstanding the monetary provisions of the U.S. Constitution. Money creation must be put squarely into the hands of the government — never mind the Constitution which is, after all, 'just a piece of paper' (with apologies to George W. Bush).

Naturally, the U.S. government and the Federal Reserve were all too eager to embrace unlimited power assigned to them by Friedman, in spite of the fact that this power was not 'enumerated' in, nay, it was explicitly denied by the Constitution of the United States. Friedman's defense of a floating currency is pseudo-scientific claptrap, modernistic stuff designed to impress the mind untrained in monetary science (as opposed to 'dismal monetary science'). The unfortunate part is that permanent damage has been inflicted to the social science faculties of our colleges and universities where so many have abandoned true science for the dismal kind, in pursuit of the scent of money.

When Friedman's monetary theory is put on a scale against the U.S. Constitution, the verdict is: Mene tekel upharsin (you have been weighed and found wanting). Why the theory in the citation for Nobel Prize not was worth to merit a constitutional amendment is an interesting story. The credentials of Friedman were not strong enough to withstand public furor that would erupt if the paper dollar, hardly worth one constitutional gold cent, was supposed to be carved into the stone of the U.S. Constitution. The powers-that-be don't want to rock the boat. It is too risky. 'Let the sleeping dog lie'. Policy-makers could not muster the necessary moral courage to initiate a constitutional amendment. They would rather live with the odium of running a blatantly unconstitutional monetary regime. Be that as it may, the next dollar crisis will force the issue.

In "Two Lucky People", written together with his wife Rose, Friedman said: "We do not influence the course of events by persuading people that we are right when we make what they regard as radical proposals. Rather, we exert influence by keeping options available when something has to be done at a time of crisis".

Well, Mr. Friedman, crisis is knocking on our door right now. It is a dollar crisis dwarfing that of 1968, or any monetary crisis in all the history of money. Do you mean to say that the option to rehabilitate the gold standard cum real bills is open still?

References

1. [1]The Real Culprit, by Walter E. Spahr, Monetary Notes, July 1, 1959.

2. [2]The Debate Is Not Over, by Walter E. Spahr, U.S.A., May 9, 1958.

3. [3]Arbeitslosigkeit und Kapitalbildung, by Heinrich Rittershausen, Jena: Fischer, 1930

4. [4]Unemployment: Human Sacrifice on the Altar of Mammon, by Antal E. Fekete, September 30, 2005

Professor, Memorial University of Newfoundland

Addemdum IV

EXPLANATION OF TERMS USED:

HUI = A basket index of shares of gold mining companies that do not forward sell (hedge) their production for periods greater than 18 months (excludes Barrick Gold, AngloGold Ashanti, etc)

TA = technical analysis, a method of determining the direction of financial markets

EWP = Elliott Wave Principle, a principle used in understanding financial markets

---

MY VIEW ON HUI AND GOLD

By Thomas Z. Tan, CFA, MBA

I have been reading many articles on the topics of gold and gold miners for a few years now. Here I would like to share my view on both gold and especially HUI, many of which are results of my own research and haven't been read from other publications. The main point of this article is if we view HUI as a derivative of gold, it will give a better understanding of HUI movement, resulting better indication and wave count than gold itself for the purpose of future projection. My forecast on gold is also discussed here.

Part One - HUI

HUI is composed of 15 large and mid size gold mining companies (with equal dollar weighting) which do not hedge beyond 1.5 years. Due to this unhedged or light hedged nature, I look at HUI more as a very long term call option of gold. As everyone knows, the best movement of HUI is from the bottom of $38 at the end of 2000 to $155 in 2002, 400 % return in 1.5 year. However, gold itself has gone only from $250 to $325 in the same period, or about 30 % return. In other words, return on HUI is over 10 times higher than gold for this period which I would call phase I, the best so far. However from

2002 to now for 4 long years, HUI is up only from \$155 to \$320, or 100 % return, in par with gold from \$325 to \$650, also 100 %. Does anyone ever ask why there is such large disparity in behavior and return between the two periods?

5-Year Weekly Chart of AMEX Gold Bugs Index.

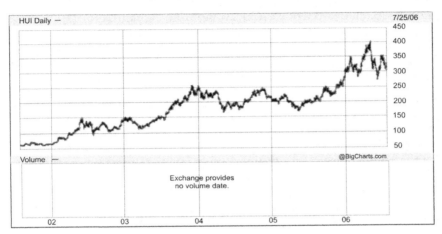

Even gold mining companies vary differently in their costs of excavating gold from ground, the average on the HUI miners is believed to be around \$325 including overhead. If you look HUI as a very long term call option of gold option (expires only when miners are in bankruptcy), it makes perfect sense why HUI return was over 10 times higher than gold in phase I. When gold reached the bottom of \$250, HUI was way out of money. Option traders know they don't worth a lot. HUI during 2000 at \$38 behaved like 100 calls (\$0.38 per call) with strike price at \$325 when gold traded at \$250, \$75 out of money. Then gold slowly rose to \$325 in the next 1.5 years and finally put HUI at the money (at its strike price), what would you think HUI should be traded at? I think \$155 per 100 calls (\$1.55 per call) would be a very reasonable market price due to the time and volatility values from the Black Scholes model. This is phase I.

Now for phase II, when gold price keeps creeping up, HUI again as a call option of gold, becomes more and more in the money, the ratio of change in HUI vs. gold is approaching one, the so-called delta hedging of a call option. That is exactly what has happened last 4 years when HUI has moved from \$155 to \$320, or 100 % return, "magically" matching gold from $325 to $650, also 100 %.

The behavior of HUI last 6 years has proved exactly that HUI is a derivative of gold, at least from a long term view. This is not a coincidence and makes perfect fundamental sense. Stock option traders know that option leads stocks, so is HUI as a leading indicator of gold.

If we accept this view, the implications are: 1) We should never view HUI independently, have to be in conjunction with gold at all time; 2) Any technical analysis (TA) on HUI alone such as Elliot Wave Projection (EWP) would only make sense if the same analysis on gold is correct; 3) The deviation of HUI from gold is a important TA indication due to its leading and lagging natures.

I have read several editorials from TA (technical analysis] standpoint that HUI will go to stratosphere by repeating the 1st phase rise from $38 to $250 in the near term. The fractal TA target is based on extrapolating the same length of movement as the previous one on a log scale. In other words, they expect the current % gain will repeat the $38-$250 run in about the same length of time. I think they will be disappointed. It is obviously incorrect to expect return of in the money calls to match out of money calls. HUI might go to stratosphere only if gold goes to stratosphere in the near future. Anything is possible in the market, but not likely (see my discussion on "Part II - Gold" below).

HUI has deviated short term from gold from time to time. The longest deviation happened and lasted for the whole year of 2004. Gold was able to creep up to a higher high but HUI couldn't and lagged behind. I think this is due to the lack of arbitrage mechanism between HUI and gold. For option arbitrage, we have something called put call parity, or c-p = S-X. For example, if call is undervalued, we can buy call, short put, short stock, buy US treasury to generate a risk free arbitrage profit. However, it is not true for HUI, since there is not a good basket of companies or index which is closely but inversely correlated to gold.

Why is the deviation in 2004 then? I think the main reason is people's expectation and perspective view on gold. At 2004, even gold rose slowly and made hew high, no one believed that gold would stay at the level of $400-$450 very long, the general public view was that gold would eventually go back down to $300-$350 level (again close to the strike price). HUI as a composition of gold miners, correctly reflected the mass view at that time by discounting the future earnings, and traded at "discount" to gold. This however won't happen in stock option due to arbitrage discussed above. It explains the following chart why HUI vs. gold ratio dropped from 0.6 to 0.4 during that period, a 33 % reduction. Will this happen today? I don't think so. The public consensus has accepted a gold price in the range between $550-$650, not far from current levels, a much more positive sentiment than in 2004.

Will HUI ever trade in "premium" to gold in the future? My view is unlikely, the reasons are: 1) Companies have too many risks such as geopolitical (foreign government, manpower, unions, environment, health & safety, regulation), reserve uncertainty, capacity limitation, management, operating issues, capital & refinancing, especially costs (as we see HUI is currently depressed by the high energy costs). 2) Reserves will eventually run out and finding and securing new reserve is always the biggest risk. If we believe that the World is running out of gold mines, this risk is huge. 3) Even if people expect gold trading at stratosphere level, unhedged gold miners can only excavate gold so much and so fast each year up to the longevity of reserves, reflecting profit or earnings based on an average gold price substantial less than the peak price. Even reserve estimate might increase with higher gold price due to low grade ore becoming profitable, but no matter what the peak gold eventually reaches, HUI will reflect a much lower average gold price due to operational constraints.

I expect in the future which I call phase III, the delta between HUI and gold will drop gradually from current 1:1 down to somewhere 0.75:1 or lower (see my chart on HUI vs. gold future correlation below). For example, when gold reaches $2000 (500 % return from $325 gold level), I only expect HUI to get to $750 (400 % return from $150 HUI level). The main reason is simply because the risk associated with owning gold is much less than all the risk associated with owning some mining companies as discussed above. I strongly believe that gold offers a better risk/reward profile than HUI, and is a better investment vehicle than HUI in the future.

However I am only talking about the large and mid tier gold miners in HUI. For small miners, exploration and early discovery companies, I view them as events driven similar to biotech firms finding drugs. If jackpot is hit by finding a new gold mine with good quality and large reserves, the return can be unimaginable, whether gold trades $1000 or $2000 makes little difference.

HUI vs. Gold

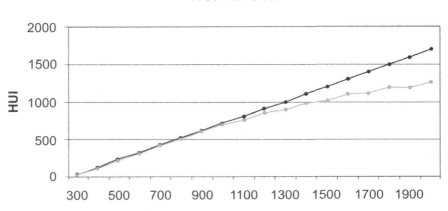

When HUI is more in the money, market will evaluate gold miners less by earnings or P/E ratios, more by the values of their reserves minus excavation costs. Analysts will use models to discount future profits from the existing reserves and will probably assign very little value of their ability to hit future jackpot due to the scarcity and low probability of finding new gold mines. I think the best return in the future is in the companies with the highest and good quality reserves. Barrick Gold's current offer to NovaGold proves this. Barrick Gold is in XAU not HUI due to its heavy hedging on gold, it makes perfect sense for a XAU hedged miner to acquire an unhedged one, increasing reserves at the same time reducing hedge.

Part Two – Gold

Since HUI basically moves with gold, I want to discuss here my view on gold's long term target and its EWP [Elliott Wave Principle]. There is no lack of such views from many resource websites, and I have learned so much from various authors, I will repeat some of them here but also give what I believe.

Long Term Gold Target

I expect gold peaks at $4000-$5000 at the end of this bull market. I agree with many people that the best way to forecast peak is by comparing gold vs. other major indexes:

1. Gold vs. DJIA. With a secular bear stock market, DJIA should drop to 5000, a 50 % reduction, the DJIA/Gold ratio could reach 1:1 at the bottom from current 18:1, thus gold at $5000.

2. Gold vs. CPI. If we use the pre-modified CPI formula prior to mid 1990s, economists have calculated the current inflation should be around 7-8 %, double the 3-4 % claimed by the government. Compounding for last 26 years, coupled with likely future higher inflation, gold should reach $3000-$4000 range to be comparable to $887.5 of 1980 dollar.

3. Gold ties more to money supply than any other factors. There is a reason why government stopped publishing M3, probably not to save $1M cost for compiling the data, but because M3 has been running out of control, rising exponentially. Economists have come up with $4000-$5000 gold in order to tie back to M3 in 1970s. Due to the lack of transparency on M3, people would think M3 is even worse than it really is (even

the real data is already bad enough). There will be a time public view greenback worthless as in the period of late 1970s to early 1980s.

4. Gold vs. Oil. At the peak, Gold vs. Oil ratio might reach 30 (not a historical all time high), putting gold to $4000 with oil at $133 or $5000 with oil at $170.

5. Gold now vs. 1970s. Gold was up from $35 to $887.5 in 1970s, 2500 % return. Using the same ratio from $250 bottom low, gold could reach over $6000.

At the same time, I have reservation on gold peak much higher than $5000 at this gold bull market. I have seen some authors projecting a gold price at $10,000 and/or higher with 5 digits. Even anything is possible in the market, but I seriously doubt 5 digits will happen in this bull market, mainly due to the ratio analysis above. Maybe it will happen in the next gold bull if someone can wait for another 40 years.

However I also believe gold will take us much higher than just the current CPI adjusted $2000 level, equivalent to $887.5 of 1980 dollar. The main fundamental reason is globalization, which brings much higher demand for gold across the globe than 1970s with more severe scarcity of gold supplies. Globalization is a double edge sword. It brings economic growth and trades but also instability for all countries alike. It exports western consumption and lifestyle to the whole World population, causing natural resource consumption increasing exponentially as well as prices for all commodities. It brings competitions to devalue paper currencies of all countries alike to gain trade advantage. If greenback as the dominant and strongest currency in the World, collapses in the future, all paper currencies will collapse together, resulting gold as the last currency standing and the only universal currency everyone can trust. Central banks (CBs) will have to compete to increase their gold reserves, developed and developing countries alike. CBs in developed countries have been net gold sellers, while CBs in all developing countries have very little gold in their reserves.

It is a pity that CBs such as Bank of England sold large shares of gold reserves at the absolute bottom of $250-$300 in 2000. From cycle standpoint, gold should have bottomed in 1999 or earlier. The early 2001 bottom according to GATA is more a manipulation and collusion of CBs than real demand and supply driven. But this kind of manipulation if true, plus discontinued M3 and new CPI "adjustments" will backfire in the future, just as $250 was an anomaly of gold at the low side, public dissatisfaction, anxiety and insecurity will cause anomaly at the other side, bringing gold to a much higher level than CPI adjusted. When Greenspan was asked by a congressman how stupid Bank of England was to sell gold at the absolute bottom, worst timing ever possible, he strongly defended them by saying "The British knew what they were doing". This led people to believe that Fed might actually involve too, maybe by lending gold or even selling at the same time, act of collusion as GATA has always suspected. No matter what happened then, three things are true: 1) Rise of gold is a nightmare for all CBs; 2) All CBs have less gold than they claim having, and will gradually have less ammunition to depress gold and eventually defenseless to protect their paper currencies; 3) At the end all CBs will have to turn into net gold buyers from sellers.

EWP [Elliott Wave Principle] of gold

This is purely based on my view on EWP. Different people have different opinions on EWP. I will give mine and I also think using EWP long term makes more sense than short term, especially in conjunction with HUI. The key here is to define where major wave II was for this gold bull after wave I started in 2001. Many people think we are currently at wave II due to the sharp drop in gold from $730-$550. I tend to disagree. If you look at HUI instead of gold from 2000, the major wave I was obvious from end of 2000 to end of 2003, lasting 3 years, while wave II was during end of 2003 to mid 2005, lasting 1.5 years (half of the time of wave I). This makes sense for EWP, all other drops are not long enough to qualify as wave II. During the same 1.5 years, gold did creep up slowly, forming a diamond shape wave II, unusual but possible and bullish for wave III. As I indicated before, EWP of HUI is more logic and accurate than gold EWP, due to both its derivative nature of gold and its ability to deviate to better reflect the real psychological level of public expectation and perspective on gold.

If my view is correct on wave II, we are currently at wave III. With wave I lasted about 3 years, wave II half of that, it is reasonable to expect wave III to last at least 2-3 years. Today wave III is only 1 year, should have at least another 1 or likely 2 more years to go until 2008, bringing us to $1800-$2000, 400 % return from wave II bottom. The current sharp drop from $730 to $550 is a necessary correction within wave III, although from the COT report, the last $50 drop from $600 to $550 was more due to manipulation by large commercials to shake the weak apples. Gold will recover sooner than expected. After wave III, I expect a serious correction of wave IV, lasting for 2 years similar to 1974-1976, bringing us down to about $1200 (50 % correction) before a run away to my final $4000-$5000 target, another 400 % gain.

If gold reaches this level as forecast, by using the same ratio of peak of $887.5 at 1980 to $250 at 2001, I project gold will bottom at $1100-$1400 as the absolute bottom at the next major gold bear market which again can last for 20 years or so. If it happens as expected, gold will still remain at 4 digits for this and next generation and probably forever as far as gold remains as the universal and last currency for the whole World. I believe once gold securely and convincingly overcomes the $1000 mark, and current wave III reaches $1800 to $2000 range, gold will never go back down below $1000, thus never be 3 digits again. When will be the best time to buy gold? Answer: If not now, when?

Thomas Z. Tan, CFA, MBA
thomast2@optonline.net

August 01, 2006

P.S. I have been reading gold and miners from various sources, trading them since 2003, and forming my opinions and analysis along the way, which have been shared with friends. Very fortunately many of my opinions have been proved correct by the market and it is probably more luck than anything else. However it gives me confidence to write this article and possible future ones to share with a much broader audience. I also want to give something back in return, especially since I have learned so much by reading articles from all of you. In this article, I tried to mix both fundamental and technical analysis for HUI and gold and give a long term view, which I feel is more reliable to share with you all than short term technical analysis which I have also involved studying. Thank you all very much.

Disclaimer: The contents of this article represent the opinion and analysis of Thomas Tan, who cannot accept responsibility for any trading losses you may incur as a result of your reliance on this opinion and analysis and will not be held liable for the consequence of reliance upon any opinion or statement contained herein or any omission. Individuals should consult with their broker and personal financial advisors before engaging in any trading activities. Do your own due diligence regarding personal investment decisions.

ADDENDUM V

President Dwight D. Eisenhower's
Farewell Speech to the Nation
January 17, 1961

My fellow Americans:

Three days from now, after half a century in the service of our country, I shall lay down the responsibilities of office as, in traditional and solemn ceremony, the authority of the Presidency is vested in my successor.

This evening I come to you with a message of leave-taking and farewell, and to share a few final thoughts with you, my countrymen.

Like every other citizen, I wish the new President, and all who will labor with him, Godspeed. I pray that the coming years will be blessed with peace and prosperity for all.

Our people expect their President and the Congress to find essential agreement on issues of great moment, the wise resolution of which will better shape the future of the Nation.

My own relations with the Congress, which began on a remote and tenuous basis when, long ago, a member of the Senate appointed me to West Point, have since ranged to the intimate during the war and immediate post-war period, and, finally, to the mutually interdependent during these past eight years.

In this final relationship, the Congress and the Administration have, on most vital issues, cooperated well, to serve the national good rather than mere partisanship, and so have assured that the business of the Nation should go forward. So, my official relationship with the Congress ends in a feeling, on my part, of gratitude that we have been able to do so much together.

II.

We now stand ten years past the midpoint of a century that has witnessed four major wars among great nations. Three of these involved our own country. Despite these holocausts America is today the strongest, the most influential and most productive nation in the world. Understandably proud of this pre-eminence, we yet realize that America's leadership and prestige depend, not merely upon our unmatched material progress, riches and military strength, but on how we use our power in the interests of world peace and human betterment.

III.

Throughout America's adventure in free government, our basic purposes have been to keep the peace; to foster progress in human achievement, and to enhance liberty, dignity and integrity among people and among nations. To strive for less would be unworthy of a free and religious people. Any failure traceable to arrogance, or our lack of comprehension or readiness to sacrifice would inflict upon us grievous hurt both at home and abroad.

Progress toward these noble goals is persistently threatened by the conflict now engulfing the world. It commands our whole attention, absorbs our very beings. We face a hostile ideology -- global in scope, atheistic in character, ruthless in purpose, and insidious in method. Unhappily the danger is poses promises to be of indefinite duration. To meet it successfully, there is called for, not so much the emotional and transitory sacrifices of crisis, but rather those which enable us to carry forward steadily, surely, and without complaint the burdens of a prolonged and complex struggle -- with liberty the stake. Only thus shall we remain, despite every provocation, on our charted course toward permanent peace and human betterment.

Crises there will continue to be. In meeting them, whether foreign or domestic, great or small, there is a recurring temptation to feel that some spectacular and costly action could become the miraculous solution to all current difficulties. A huge increase in newer elements of our defense; development of unrealistic programs to cure every ill in agriculture; a dramatic expansion in basic and applied research -- these and many other possibilities, each possibly promising in itself, may be suggested as the only way to the road we wish to travel.

But each proposal must be weighed in the light of a broader consideration: the need to maintain balance in and among national programs -- balance between the private and the public economy, balance between cost and hoped for advantage -- balance between the clearly necessary and the comfortably desirable; balance between our essential requirements as a nation and the duties imposed by the nation upon the individual; balance between actions of the moment and the national welfare of the future. Good judgment seeks balance and progress; lack of it eventually finds imbalance and frustration.

The record of many decades stands as proof that our people and their government have, in the main, understood these truths and have responded to them well, in the face of stress and threat. But threats, new in kind or degree, constantly arise. I mention two only.

IV.

A vital element in keeping the peace is our military establishment. Our arms must be mighty, ready for instant action, so that no potential aggressor may be tempted to risk his own destruction.

Our military organization today bears little relation to that known by any of my predecessors in peacetime, or indeed by the fighting men of World War II or Korea.

Until the latest of our world conflicts, the United States had no armaments industry. American makers of plowshares could, with time and as required, make swords as well. But now we can no longer risk emergency improvisation of national defense; we have been compelled to create a permanent armaments industry of vast proportions. Added to this, three and a half million men and women are directly engaged in the defense establishment. We annually spend on military security more than the net income of all United States corporations.

This conjunction of an immense military establishment and a large arms industry is new in the American experience. The total influence -- economic, political, even spiritual -- is felt in every city, every State house, every office of the Federal government. We recognize the imperative need for this development. Yet we must not fail to comprehend its grave implications. Our toil, resources and livelihood are all involved; so is the very structure of our society.

In the councils of government, we must guard against the acquisition of unwarranted influence, whether sought or unsought, by the militaryindustrial complex. The potential for the disastrous rise of misplaced power exists and will persist.

We must never let the weight of this combination endanger our liberties or democratic processes. We should take nothing for granted. Only an alert and knowledgeable citizenry can compel the proper meshing of the huge industrial and military machinery of defense with our peaceful methods and goals, so that security and liberty may prosper together.

Akin to, and largely responsible for the sweeping changes in our industrial-military posture, has been the technological revolution during recent decades.

In this revolution, research has become central; it also becomes more formalized, complex, and costly. A steadily increasing share is conducted for, by, or at the direction of, the Federal government.

Today, the solitary inventor, tinkering in his shop, has been overshadowed by task forces of scientists in laboratories and testing fields. In the same fashion, the free university, historically the fountainhead of free ideas and scientific discovery, has experienced a revolution in the conduct of research. Partly because of the huge costs involved, a government contract becomes virtually a substitute for intellectual curiosity. For every old blackboard there are now hundreds of new electronic computers.

The prospect of domination of the nation's scholars by Federal employment, project allocations, and the power of money is ever present and is gravely to be regarded.

Yet, in holding scientific research and discovery in respect, as we should, we must also be alert to the equal and opposite danger that public policy could itself become the captive of a scientifictechnological elite.

It is the task of statesmanship to mold, to balance, and to integrate these and other forces, new and old, within the principles of our democratic system -- ever aiming toward the supreme goals of our free society.

V.

Another factor in maintaining balance involves the element of time. As we peer into society's future, we -- you and I, and our government -- must avoid the impulse to live only for today, plundering, for our own ease and convenience, the precious resources of tomorrow. We cannot mortgage the material assets of our grandchildren without risking the loss also of their political and spiritual heritage. We want democracy to survive for all generations to come, not to become the insolvent phantom of tomorrow.

VI.

Down the long lane of the history yet to be written America knows that this world of ours, ever growing smaller, must avoid becoming a community of dreadful fear and hate, and be instead, a proud confederation of mutual trust and respect.

Such a confederation must be one of equals. The weakest must come to the conference table with the same confidence as do we, protected as we are by our moral, economic, and military strength. That table, though scarred by many past frustrations, cannot be abandoned for the certain agony of the battlefield.

Disarmament, with mutual honor and confidence, is a continuing imperative. Together we must learn how to compose differences, not with arms, but with intellect and decent purpose. Because this need is so sharp and apparent I confess that I lay down my official responsibilities in this field with a definite sense of disappointment. As one who has witnessed the horror and the lingering sadness of war -- as one who knows that another war could utterly destroy this civilization which has been so slowly and painfully built over thousands of years -- I wish I could say tonight that a lasting peace is in sight.

Happily, I can say that war has been avoided. Steady progress toward our ultimate goal has been made. But, so much remains to be done. As a private citizen, I shall never cease to do what little I can to help the world advance along that road.

VII.

So -- in this my last good night to you as your President -- I thank you for the many opportunities you have given me for public service in war and peace. I trust that in that service you find some things worthy; as for the rest of it, I know you will find ways to improve performance in the future.

You and I -- my fellow citizens -- need to be strong in our faith that all nations, under God, will reach the goal of peace with justice. May we be ever unswerving in devotion to principle, confident but humble with power, diligent in pursuit of the Nation's great goals.

To all the peoples of the world, I once more give expression to America's prayerful and continuing aspiration:

We pray that peoples of all faiths, all races, all nations, may have their great human needs satisfied; that those now denied opportunity shall come to enjoy it to the full; that all who yearn for freedom may experience its spiritual blessings; that those who have freedom will understand, also, its heavy responsibilities; that all who are insensitive to the needs of others will learn charity; that the scourges of poverty, disease and ignorance will be made to disappear from the earth, and that, in the goodness of time, all peoples will come to live together in a peace guaranteed by the binding force of mutual respect and love.

ADDENDUM VI

It Will Get Better; But, First, It's Going To Get Worse

Humanity is moving ever deeper into crisis—a crisis without precedent.
- Buckminster Fuller, 1981

For the past three hundred years, history has been influenced by economics, most importantly by capitalism. After the rise of communism, capitalism became primarily identified with "free-markets".

The identification with "free markets' was a public relations coup for capitalism that would have made the Rothschilds, the Morgans, and the banking elites proud. It was also a distortion of the truth.

Free markets existed before capitalism appeared in the 18th century. Capitalism is an economic system where the bankers' capital, i.e. debt-based paper banknotes, are substituted for money and issued in the form of credit. This marked departure from savings-based money, i.e. gold or silver, allowed bankers to charge interest on paper banknotes, a far more lucrative business than charging interest on gold and silver.

The ability to issue debt-based paper money as loans, first in England then around the world, allowed bankers to eventually indebt all countries; and, now, three hundred years later the entire world uses debt-based capital as money and has become indebted beyond the ability to repay.

The very success of capitalism has led to its demise. The sovereign debt crisis that has consumed Europe since 2010 is about to spread to the US, the UK, Japan and other nations where debts are now so large they can only be repaid by printing even more paper banknotes.

The collapse of capitalism will be far more significant than the collapse of communism. Capitalism's effect on the world was profound and its passing will be as well. Today's world, tenuously balanced between massive levels of credit and debt, has begun to tilt dangerously towards defaulting debt as central bankers try to restore the balance between the two by making even more credit available.

The bankers' efforts will be futile. The present age is passing and a new age is about to take its place. A paradigm shift of immeasurable importance is in motion. One which Buckminster Fuller predicted would be ushered in by a crisis that would be unprecedented in nature.

My advice to transfer paper-based wealth to either gold or silver is based on my belief that capitalism's fall will be cataclysmic in the extreme. Paradigm shifts of this magnitude are often accompanied by episodes of social disorder, chaos, inflation and natural disasters.

Weather patterns are becoming extreme and such phenomena are not unexpected during such times. David Hackett Fisher characterized the present shift as a sea-change in change itself. He's right and so is Buckminster Fuller.

Both Fisher and Fuller believe that the succeeding epoch will be better than the present era; and Fuller is the most optimistic of the two. Fuller believes the crisis is cosmically intended to *transform humanity into a completely integrated, comprehensively interconsiderate, harmonious whole.*

This crisis involves far more than money. Our thinking is caught up in the demise of the present paradigm and we cannot yet imagine the world that is to come. There is no need to do so. It will come in its own time and will be far different than anything we can even imagine.

It Will Get Better; But, First, It's Going To Get Worse.

Buy gold, buy silver, have faith.

Good luck and Godspeed.

Darryl Robert Schoon

July 2012

Books by Darryl Robert Schoon

Light in a Dark Place – The Prison Years (2006, 2nd Ed. 2012)
Darryl Robert Schoon's stories, poetry and essays are political, spiritual, always human and, at times, enlightened. "Darryl's voice is one that at times seems to tap into the very soul of the universe" (Marshall Thurber, founder of the Positive Deviant Network). Light in a Dark Place tells the story of Howard Hughes' banker who gave details of a Reagan White House skim of Saudi funds. The funds were discovered in a CIA Swiss bank account controlled by an Israeli banker later linked to 9/11. These links shed light on why 9/11 happened.

Time of the Vulture: How to Survive the Crisis and Prosper in the Process (2007, 2009, 3rd Ed. 2012)
This book predicted in 2007 why an economic crisis of unexpected magnitude and consequences was about to occur and was updated in 2012. Bought by readers in 25 countries, e.g. the US, UK, Australia, China, Switzerland, France, Paraguay, etc., it explains the nature of the crisis and ways to survive and profit.

You Can't Always Get What You Want – a novel (2012)
"Who do you think you are anyhow? At least I know I'm in a cage." The words of the monkey are never forgotten as the protagonist pursues dreams of romance on his way to Paris in a tension-filled novel of intrigue, danger and deception.

Is God Confused? – thoughts on the human condition (2012)
God isn't confused. Man is confused. This book explains mankind's predicament and the solution. Darryl Robert Schoon's spiritual observations on life are as uniquely penetrating as his observations about bankers and money.

The Way to Heaven – thoughts on the human condition (2012)
The way to heaven isn't easy but it's a lot easier than staying as you are; and the sooner you start, the sooner you'll arrive. Judgments will keep us in hell; forgiveness will lead us to heaven.

These books can be ordered at **www.drschoon.com**.